At Home in the World

❖

At HOME
in the
WORLD

A Rule of Life for the Rest of Us

Margaret Guenther

SEABURY BOOKS
an imprint of
Church Publishing Incorporated, New York

*For "the rest of us" —
my beloved community of St. Columba*

Library of Congress Cataloging-in-Publication Data

Guenther, Margaret, 1930–
At home in the world : a rule of life for the rest of us /
Margaret Guenther
        p. cm.
Includes bibliographical references.
ISBN 1-59627-026-8
ISBN13 978-1-59627-026-8

1. Spiritual life—Christianity. 2. Spirituality. I. Title.
BV4501.3.G84 2006
248.4—dc22

                                                    2006006028

Cover photograph © Simon Brown

Church Publishing, Incorporated
445 Fifth Avenue
New York, New York 10016
www.churchpublishing.org

Contents

Acknowledgments

Although writing is a profoundly solitary act, no book writes itself. I am deeply grateful for the help and friendship of my editors, Cynthia Shattuck and Vicki Black.

I have been supported also by the generous hospitality of the Benedictine communities that have welcomed me as sister and friend. As always, I have been sustained and encouraged by my family: my husband Jack, my children, and my grandchildren.

To all of you—a heartfelt thank you.

part 1
Why a Rule?

Rules,
Roots, and Branches

❖❖ When I was a small child, I knew a song from my grandparents' days: "School days, school days, dear old golden rule days; reading and writing and 'rithmetic taught to the tune of a hickory stick." I liked it and disliked it simultaneously. The tune was lilting, and the severe pedagogic regimen safely in the past, yet the linking of the Golden Rule and that stick was too close for comfort.

In our four-room school desks were clamped to the floor in neat rows, fastened to sturdy metal strips like miniature railroad tracks. Window shades were impeccably aligned—woe to the teacher whose blinds were out of sync. No talking unless you held up your hand, no whispering, no gum-chewing, no getting up from your seat without permission: pencil sharpening was an exciting diversion, and an authorized trip to the basement bathroom a high point in the day. You formed a neat line to go to the playground, where boys played on one side of the squat brick building and girls on the other. I once had to carry a message to the teacher on duty on the boys' side and felt as if I were doing something dangerously illicit.

Would I be praised for efficient delivery of the message, or reproached for being in forbidden territory?

This was not a harsh environment. The children were not struck or shouted at. All the rules were in fact reassuring, probably like the rules of a benevolent prison: you knew exactly where you were supposed to be and what you were to be doing at any given moment. But the rules were not freely chosen by the small inmates: they were a given, handed down by remote authorities. Spontaneity had no place, nor did exuberant creativity. Who knows what might have happened if some rampaging free spirit had tried to blossom among us docile children in the 1930s in the neighborhood called Rosedale?

Rules—they structure and punctuate our lives. There is the rule of the road and the rule of law. There are rules of grammar, happily ignored by many. Some rulers are heads of state; some are twelve-inch strips of wood or plastic tucked in the middle desk drawer. There are even three saints named "Rule." My favorite is St. Regula, martyred in 302 and now remembered as one of the patrons of hyper-Protestant Zurich. Beheaded, she carried her severed head to an ancient church on the riverbank, where she deposited it to mark one of the future cornerstones. St. Rule was an obscure fourth-century Scottish saint reputed to have brought relics of St. Andrew to Scotland. He is not to be confused with St. Regulus of Senlis—I haven't managed to find out who he was. Nor have I found any indication of how these saints got their names. Were they sticklers for doing things decently and in order, or did they compose rules for their communities? Or were they stragglers and underachievers who needed the structure of a rule to hold them up?

Not long ago, looking for something else, I found a folder labeled "Rule" in my computer directory. It is not a folder that I had created, but lies buried among those innumerable indecipherable items on the hard drive. It contains seventeen forbidding-looking files that obviously have something to do with the continued healthy functioning of my desktop. Like my three enigmatic saints, I haven't a clue how it got its name, nor can I fathom what its purpose might be. Now that I know it's there, I will continue to keep my distance and treat it with a healthy respect.

❖ *Contemporary Rules*

In the freedom-loving twenty-first century I find myself wanting to write a book about rules. Not just those ordinary practical rules that help us get through the day—stand to the right and walk on the left on an escalator, put the trash out Tuesday night, take your laptop out of the case before going through security while juggling your shoes. And not those rules that restrict and oppress us, that compel us to plod when we really want to dance. I am convinced that, even as we celebrate freedom, we yearn for rules. It is frightening and disorienting to be adrift. Any parent of small children knows that structure is essential. Children find it liberating to know when they will eat and when they will sleep, to know clearly which behaviors are acceptable and which are not, to know that they are protected from danger. There are times when life itself may depend on knowing and observing the rules. At the very least, there is freedom and security when our days are shaped and held by a supportive structure. Further, any terrorist—international, domestic, or household—knows that uncertainty is the most powerful weapon.

Even as we might resist rules imposed by others as blighting our promise and hampering our creativity, we seek them out and cling to them like drowning swimmers to a lifeline. In our well-fed society, many of these rules currently constellate around the intake of food. In simpler times counting calories could become an obsession; then in the 1980s came the promise of eating more and weighing less. For fruit and vegetable-lovers this permissive approach was almost too easy, so fat was banished, then "bad" carbohydrates, then seemingly *all* carbohydrates.

Current dietary rules have come to rival the precepts set forth in the book of Leviticus. So now when I share a meal with Atkins diet aficionados, I am reproached by my own lack of self-discipline. As I drop a little balsamic vinegar on my salad, I envy their clarity, their understanding of the acceptable and the forbidden.

Our very identities seem determined by our dietary regimens. I may not know who is Episcopalian or Presbyterian, Conservative or Reformed, Democrat or Republican, but even short and relatively casual acquaintance can make clear who is Atkins or South Beach, low carb or no carb, organic or conventional, vegan or lacto-ovarian. I cannot resist pondering the roots of such dedicated asceticism. People of faith who are casual in their religious observance and neglectful of the spiritual disciplines can become rigorous to the point of zealotry about their carbs or workouts. Rigid observance of a rule, not imposed but freely chosen, can provide a feeling of safety. I find myself remembering a childhood rule, faithfully observed and passed on by oral tradition: "Don't step on a crack or you'll break your mother's back." Did we avoid the cracks in the sidewalk because we loved our mothers and feared what would happen to us without them? Or did we feel power over the most powerful person in our lives, power that we resisted even as we contemplated it? Or were we just having fun, adding shape to the repetitive work of walking to and from school every day?

The prevailing rule of our time finds its roots in Ohio, where Alcoholics Anonymous, the parent of all the twelve-step programs, was born in 1935. These programs have burgeoned in the decades since: a cursory surfing of the Internet yields dozens of self-help programs based on the principles of AA, revealing the wide range of addictive behaviors in our addicted society. Could we be addicted to addiction? Or might addiction simply be a new way of looking at idolatry, and the deceptively simple twelve steps be a new articulation of ancient spiritual truths?

Is it merely graced coincidence that in his rule for monastic communities Benedict describes the twelve degrees of humility? Twelve is, after all, a significant if not mystical number: there are twelve days of Christmas, twelve tribes of Israel, twelve apostles, and twelve months in a year. Why not twelve steps on the path to wholeness? The steps themselves have a decidedly monastic ring, succinct and deceptively simple: I admit my need of God, I choose to believe that God is able to restore me to sanity, and I turn my life over to God's care. As an ongoing spiritual discipline I make a searching "moral inventory" of my life and confess my wrongdoings, asking for forgiveness and restoration, and making restitution where possible. I seek to know God through prayer and meditation, asking for the power to carry out God's will in every part of my life and making an effort to share my experience of God with others.

I found it an illuminating exercise to read an Alcoholics Anonymous publication from 1952 simultaneously with the Rule of St. Benedict and the even older Rule of St Augustine. The similarities were striking: the twelve steps, a deeply personal confession of sin, repentance, and commitment, are articulated in the first-person plural: it is "we" not "I" who acknowledge powerlessness and the need to change. The hard work of conversion, which is the drastic redirection of one's life, is not to be undertaken alone. Whether in a medieval monastery or a twelve-step group meeting in the church basement, the rule is read and re-read constantly in the gathered community. The seeker after God is always on the way; the addict is always recovering, not yet recovered. Even the ideal of monastic poverty is foundational in the twelve-step ethos, where the extraneous has been stripped away in anonymity and admission of powerlessness is the great leveler.

The founders of the twelve-step programs were concerned quite literally with saving lives: only God—the higher Power—could restore them to *sanity*. We associate this word primarily with mental or emotional health, but its roots are much deeper. Sanity is wholeness, health, salvation, which is the goal of the great monastic rules. Even when attention is given to the most detailed matters, the vision is expansive and life-giving.

❖ *Traditional Rules*

The Rule of St. Benedict is a bestseller today. Monasteries offer "Benedictine experiences," retreats in which participants live for a few days according to the rhythm of the Rule. A number of business and management websites promise to present Benedictine principles in "a fresh and original way that is applicable to any manager or organization today"; some promote the Rule as a source of "classic management secrets you can use today." I tried to imagine a fast-food restaurant or a used car dealership run on Benedictine principles. As one monk I know, himself a Benedictine, remarked to me wryly, "We could even sell laundry detergent if we labeled it 'Benedictine.'" Yet Benedict's Rule deserves its popularity, especially among those of us who are trying to find our way in a complex and overstimulated world.

Antedating the Benedict's Rule by two centuries, Augustine's Rule is presumed to have been written shortly after he became bishop of Hippo. When he had to leave the monastery that he had established to assume his episcopal duties, Augustine set down in writing the advice that he could no longer give personally. Like Benedict's, his Rule was written for a group of diverse men living a life of prayer in community. It is very brief, offering precepts to be observed rather than particular rules for specific situations. Indeed, the word "rule" *(regula)* does not appear in the document.[1] Not so well-known as Benedict's, it too provides insight into monastic life of long ago and offers equally important guidance for the rest of us.

Not all the traditional rules are directed at large communities of men. One of my favorite books from the high

Middle Ages is the *Ancrene Wisse,* written in the early decades of the thirteenth century in Middle English, the language of Chaucer and Julian of Norwich. The author, an anonymous priest, wrote it as a guide for three anchorites, women who lived as solitaries in cells attached to parish churches. In some ways they were the spiritual descendants of the holy—if bizarre—fathers of the Egyptian desert, deliberately cutting themselves off from the world and living in great austerity. But there were significant differences: the anchoress lived right in the heart of the town in a little room attached to the parish church, dead to the world yet very much a part of it. The ritual of her entry into the anchorhold was in part a burial liturgy. Once she entered her cell, the door was barred on the outside, and she never returned to "the world"—even though it was only a few feet away.

Her dwelling, more like a modest efficiency apartment than a stark cell, had three windows: one into the church, so that she could observe the celebration of the Eucharist and receive the sacrament; one into her garden—yes, she had a garden and a servant to tend it; and one opening onto the street. This was the vulnerable window, a vital link to others and at the same time a dangerous temptation. Through it she could speak to women who sought her spiritual counsel and to priests who would hear her confession, but she had to be careful to keep her hands inside and not to show her face.

I come back to that odd, fascinating old book again and again because those anchorites have something to teach the rest of us about the discipline of following a rule. They lived their lives of prayer and work without bells to call them to the chapel at the appointed hours, without the support and example of a community, and—this might have been hardest of all—without the benevolent and sometimes ominous oversight of an abbess. Similarly, for most of us most of the time, the inner journey is a solitary one.

The anchorite's rule was twofold: an inner and an outer rule. Not really a rule *per se,* it was more a set of guidelines. The aim of the anchoritic life, painfully cramped and restricted by our standards, was an expanded inner world. The outer rule dealt with externals: food, clothing, work, hours of prayer, and permissible contact with others. It was flexible, according to circumstances, and existed only to serve the inner rule. As the anonymous author explains, it

> is entirely concerned with outward things, and rules the body and bodily actions. This teaches everything about how a person should behave outwardly—how to eat, drink, dress, sing, sleep, keep vigil.... And this rule exists only to serve the other. The other is like the lady, this like her handmaid. For all that a person ever does according to the latter, outwardly, is only to rule the heart within.[2]

The purpose of the inner rule was purity of heart, a single-minded focus on the love of God. For this the author offers no recipe, no easy set of ten rules or twelve steps. It is a powerful reminder of what we are about when we seek solitude as a spiritual practice. The externals are not really important: we might choose a religious house or a solitary cabin in the mountains; we might participate in a structured retreat or go off on our own; we might be helped to move into the silence by carefully chosen music, or we might find music distracting. And on and on—the possibilities are myriad. More broadly, for those of us not called to actual solitude, the *Ancrene Wisse* has a powerful message: it is the purpose, the intent of our rule that matters, not the externals.

In many ways, it is all a matter of translation—not just moving the words from medieval Latin or Middle English into the English of our day, but also uncovering the verities and commonalities in the lives of faithful people throughout the ages. When I read in Benedict's Rule that the monk who ends his week of service in the kitchen must "wash the towels with which his brethren have wiped their hands and feet," my first thought is that I would

rather not eat in the monastic refectory—I could just picture those towels by the end of the week! When I translate
this precept from a medieval monastery to the typical
parish kitchen, however, it seems very wise and practical
indeed. Clean up after yourself! Leave the place tidy! If
Benedict were writing now, he might urge cleaning out
that parish refrigerator at the end of your tour of duty; it
is no place to grow penicillin on old cucumbers. Wipe up
spills, and return everything to its proper place. Maybe
even wash the towels.

The specifics of the old rules may seem austere and
confining. I am quite happy, for example, that I am not, like
Augustine's monks, compelled to relinquish my summer
wardrobe to the keeper of the clothes when September
comes and then to receive my winter garments willy-nilly
from the common closet, wondering in advance what
shapeless, badly-fitting outfit I will be given in May. I am
quite happy that unlike the anchoress I am free to talk to
all sorts of men, not just the occasional passing priest, and
to lean boldly out the window. Yet once we move past the
details, it is clear that the traditional monastic values of
poverty, chastity, and obedience are not outmoded con-
cepts, even though they seem out of place in the mall.

Current monastic rules are usually "in house" documents, but the Society of Saint John the Evangelist in
Cambridge, Massachusetts, has generously made its rule
available to the wider community. Gracefully written, each
of the forty-nine brief chapters invites reflection. Although
they deal with the structure of an Episcopal men's monastic community, they are remarkably relevant for the rest of
us. As the authors comment:

> From the very beginning of this movement in the church
> there have been many of us who are not called actually
> to belong to a religious community but who have a deep
> sense of sharing in the monastic spirit and values. This is

the phenomenon of 'interiorized monasticism,' to use a phrase of the Eastern Church.[3]

How comforting it is for the rest of us to have a name for the object of our quest and our yearning! A good rule is not a complicated "how-to" manual, but a sheltering and sustaining *place*. A refuge—not for hiding or avoidance, but for gathering strength.

❖ *Why Follow a Rule?*

Consciously or unconsciously, we all follow a rule. Unstated, unarticulated rules can make our lives run smoothly, efficiently, and predictably: my health is better and my work more fruitful if I sleep seven hours a night, eat my vegetables, and remember to say my prayers. On the other hand, our unconscious rules can be rigid and destructive. Fear of risk can paralyze us: "We've always done it this way" is one such mantra. Or we can even forget why we are following a rule. For years I placed a sheet of cookies on the upper shelf of the oven until halfway through baking, then moved it to the lower shelf. Why? My mother baked that way. I'm not sure when I figured out that she had adapted her method to our temperamental old oven, and that my cookies would do just fine if they stayed where I had put them in the first place.

I suspect that all of us have some unarticulated rule of life that enables us to get through the day as good stewards of our time and energy, getting done what needs to be done with reasonable efficiency. We may not think a great deal about it, but it shapes our days. I can think of nothing worse than floundering in a sea of minutes and hours, trying to do three things at once and doing none of them reasonably well. Should I brush my teeth or plug in the coffeepot or write my lecture? Perhaps I should make a phone call or maybe check the morning news on Channel 4 or maybe write that thank-you note I have been putting off. Some structure to the day, rigid or casual depending on our temperament, keeps us on track.

We may also follow a rule to achieve a long-term goal. To earn a degree requires years of following the rules set down by an impersonal institution. As I look back on my checkered academic past, I marvel at my tenacity and humility: to earn a degree in German literature, where the twentieth century was my chosen field, I doggedly mastered the intricacies of obscure and now defunct medieval dialects, not because such knowledge was remotely useful to me but because it had been decreed a requirement by a long-forgotten pedant. The only remnant of my linguistic struggles is the ability to recite the Lord's Prayer in Gothic, a language that can rarely be worked into a conversation. Some of these rules that we would never choose for ourselves are helpful, some are not, but they mark our paths of achievement.

We follow a rule, too, when we wish to produce something, whether we are building a boat or baking a cake. Old-fashioned cookbooks spoke of recipes as "rules." Nowadays I am a rather casual cook, probably because over the decades the rules have written themselves somewhere on my culinary internal hard drive and I know what I can get away with. It would be quite another matter if I decided to build a computer or even to assemble my own computer desk. I did manage to put together a small bookcase once—it took only several hours of following illegible instructions and some frustration when peg A refused to fit into hole A; the bookcase wobbles only slightly and seems strong enough if treated tenderly. If I had not followed the rules, though, I would have been left with a few odd boards and some bits and pieces of hardware.

A thoughtful rule of life is quite another matter. Even when it deals with the small things in our lives, a rule of life is never trivial. It cannot be coerced; it must be voluntary. Prisoners, conscripts to the military, refugees in camps, even the biddable children of my early school days all live under a rule that they have not chosen. A voluntary rule is different; it has a life-giving freedom even when it seems restrictive to outsiders.

Several years ago I led a retreat whose theme was "I am the vine, and you are the branches." *What on earth can I find new to say about those very familiar words?* I wondered. Instead of turning to the Bible commentaries, I took myself off to the local Barnes and Noble and got a few books on viticulture. It was fascinating. From my study of the cultivation of grapes two important things have stayed with me. First, all grapes need trellises if they are to bear much fruit, and there are many ways to build a trellis, depending on the variety of grape and the growing conditions. After all, not all grapes are alike; they need different kinds of support. Creating a rule of life is like that: what liberates one person may constrict another.

Likewise, what serves me well at this stage of my life would have been quite wrong, even damaging, for me as a twenty-year-old. From my viticulture book I also learned that growers of grapes know that the vine must not be tied too tightly to the trellis, but just snugly enough so that it is supported and free to flourish. Like the vines, we too need to be supported but not constricted, held up but not rendered immobile.

Making a rule, like devising a trellis, must have something to do with real people trying to get through their days mindfully and fruitfully. The very phrase "rule of life" suggests something far removed from modern life, and there is always the danger of romanticizing the past and seeking to live by an unreal and absurd standard that cannot be maintained. A rule of life for the rest of us has to be rooted in the here-and-now; it has to be germane and useful. But for Christians seeking to cultivate a life with God and one another, the classic monastic rules are a good place to begin.

2

Preparing the Vineyard

I confess that I enjoy going to monasteries. When I have retreated for a few days to a religious house and the bell rings for the first prayers of the day at what seems to me an ungodly hour, I sometimes show up in the chapel, fully dressed and alert, feeling quite holy. But more often I listen to the bell and then roll over, lulled back to sleep by the comforting thought that my sisters or brothers have begun their day's work of prayer and my services are not needed. I know that I am a guest, treated to be sure like family, and that my participation in the structured life of the community is temporary. So even as I love and am nurtured by my relationship with a number of monastic communities, I am not a nun.

Furthermore, I assume that the "rest of us," those of you who are reading this book, are just like me. We are ordinary people, yearning—perhaps unconsciously—for deep and meaningful structure in our lives in a world that is fast-paced and swarming with distractions. Like my monastic friends, we too live under vows: our baptismal vows, which are quite formidable if we take them seriously; and for many of us, our marriage vows, equally formidable. But we are ordinary, fallible people living ordinary, untidy lives that are, paradoxically, too often tightly and rigidly scheduled even as we feel overwhelmed and lost in linear time. If we let ourselves be creative translators, the wisdom of centuries very different from ours can be a friendly guide. The ancient vows—the vows of poverty, chastity, and obedience, stability and conversion of life—that bound quite disparate men (and later, women) into communities may seem remote, quaint, harsh, even impossible. At the very least, they do not seem to be relevant for us. Yet if we look at them with new eyes, if we strip away their medieval trappings, we can see that they might have something to say to ordinary people like us, as we try to live fruitfully and harmoniously with one another. I am encouraged to remember that my monastic forebears were ordinary people too, imperfect like us. Faithfulness to their vows was not a magic path to perfection; rather, it provided a strong foundation for the living of their lives. The vows were like a road map, showing them the way. But it was up to them to put one foot in front of the other, sometimes skipping, sometimes dancing, sometimes just walking, and sometimes plodding painfully.

❖ *Recovering Asceticism as a Way of Life*
To most of us the word "asceticism" suggests a life of self-inflicted misery and harsh deprivation—grim stuff indeed. In America we live in a society where self-indulgence is close to being a civic duty if we are to sustain the economy, and even our poor are well-off by world standards. The idea of deliberate self-denial is alien: you will not find hair shirts at Nordstrom's, and the portions at McDonald's are not conducive to serious fasting. So perhaps it is time to reclaim asceticism, to ponder what it really is, how it might even be conducive to our physical and spiritual health. In other words, it's time to strip away our distorted assumptions. How can we go about it, and who will help us?

Asceticism as we understand it today does not enter the picture until the early church. In a well-known passage in his first letter to the Corinthians, Paul describes the purpose of *askesis:* it is not masochistic self-punishment, but rather a matter of being in shape. His is the language of the trainer, the coach, who asks nothing more of his followers than he demands of himself:

> You know (do you not?) that at the sports all the runners run the race, though only one wins the prize. Like them, run to win! But every athlete goes into strict training. They do it to win a fading wreath; we, a wreath that never fades. (1 Corinthians 9:24–25, NEB)

Paul is writing to a young church in Corinth, a city of great ethnic and religious diversity with a reputation for moral laxity that alarmed the less cosmopolitan folk of the early Christian world. In Paul's view, these church members are arrogant and self-indulgent. He writes to them with severity, but also with great affection. These are not easy people, but they are worth bothering with. They need their priorities straightened out, and they need toughening up spiritually if they are to survive. Asceticism, as proclaimed by Paul, is no more stringent than many of our current regimens for physical fitness. At its very simplest, it is a matter of stewardship: what are those ways of living and being that will lead to the ultimate prize, the wreath that does not fade?

So it was after Paul's time and after the Roman persecutions ceased that severe, self-punishing ascetic practices came to be regarded as signs of great holiness. After all, if one had risked torture and death for following Christ, there was no need to adopt special spiritual disciplines as a test of devotion. Just getting through the day was probably enough. So asceticism earned its bad name among the fathers (and few mothers) of the Egyptian desert of the fifth century. Their sayings make fascinating reading, especially after a hearty meal and a few glasses of wine! It is clear that some of them were extraordinarily wise and devout, but I suspect that quite a few were cranky—how could they not be if they were hungry, tired, thirsty, unwashed, and isolated?—and some were probably quite mad.

Beginning with the holy people of the desert and continuing through the Middle Ages, the body itself became the problem, if not the enemy. The fourteenth century provides an especially rich source of ascetic excesses. Catherine of Siena is the best-known of holy women who purportedly lived for long periods on nothing but communion bread. Dorothea of Montau fasted to the point of death, until her confessor intervened, and then she subdued her flesh by flagellating herself until her back looked like "a plowed field." Her contemporary, Heinrich Seuse, devised a garment with a hundred and fifty sharp brass nails pointing inward, which he wore as a nightshirt until, after sixteen years, an angel appeared to him and whispered that God wanted him to discontinue the practice. He then threw the shirt into the Rhine. His biographers do not tell us whether he experienced relief or regret as it sank from sight.

Perhaps it is no accident that the Rule of St. Benedict, foundational to Anglican spirituality and timeless in its balanced wisdom, offered a humane corrective. With Benedict's help we can look to a recovery of asceticism as a way of life that promotes health and wholeness. The title of the Quaker writer Richard Foster's best-known book, *Celebration of Discipline: The Path to Spiritual Growth,* is refreshing but a bit jolting. "Celebration," after all, suggests having a good time, while "discipline" makes me sit up a little straighter. Yet the subtitle makes clear that the goal of ascetical practice is growth, that discipline is not an end in itself, but a helper to be celebrated. As Margaret Miles reminds us in *Fullness of Life: Historical Foundations of a New Asceticism,* the purpose of all ascetical disciplines is an increased self-understanding, the overcoming of habituation and addiction, the gathering and focusing of energy, an ability to change our cultural condition, and a renewed consciousness. Could we twenty-first-century people be just as well-intended but as wildly off the mark as Dorothea with her life-threatening fasts and Heinrich with his unique nightshirt?

❖ Mutual Obedience

Poverty... chastity... obedience... stability... conversion of life. Strong old words that suggest an austere life in an underheated, starkly furnished building without recliners, freezers, or hot showers. Yet these promises are foundational to the classic rules of the religious life. Three vows are basic to Benedictine spirituality: obedience, stability, and *conversatio morum* (usually translated as "conversion of life").

True obedience is a gift we bring to each other in love. And it is related—if we trace it back to its Latin roots—to a strong, ordinary little word: *audire,* to hear. Obedience is to be lovingly present and attentive to another; to hear, truly to hear what the other is saying, with words and sometimes without. We owe obedience to all those whom we love and who love us. It is the ground for any fruitful relationship. We owe obedience to all those with whom we live in covenanted relationships. Hurtful things cannot thrive, but all kinds of good things can flourish when we are carefully attentive to one another.

Willing obedience distinguishes a good working environment. A few years ago I had the luxury of a very competent administrative assistant. Eve kept my calendar straight, was gracious and helpful to all comers, and a hard and cheerful worker with one exception: she hated to photocopy papers! Each time as she departed for the copy room with a sheaf of papers in her hands, she would turn to me in mock outrage and announce, "I hate this, you know." Then we would both laugh. We were indeed mutually attentive, and she knew that I valued her gifts and her loyalty. We both knew, too, that there was a certain amount of drudgery to be got through, and Eve knew that I did my share—even though I sometimes left her stuck with mountains of copying.

Generous mutual obedience can be the glue that holds a marriage together in uneasy times of transition. It may manifest itself in the compromises that dot the years, often unrecognized and unacknowledged at the time. In a healthy marriage, both partners have abundant opportunity to take their turns, to redirect their steps toward a path that they would not have not chosen for themselves. Domestic routine often receives a jolt when the primary parent returns to school or a new job. Where will the tuition money come from? Will favorite family dishes be replaced by pizza and Chinese takeout? And what will it be like for the rest of the household when the caregiver's world expands so drastically that they are no longer the absolute center?

As Parker Palmer writes in *To Know as We Are Known: The Spirituality of Education,* obedience also lies at the heart of fruitful learning, where teacher and student are pledged to obedience to each other and to truth itself. As a student, I would work prodigiously and cheerfully for any teacher dedicated to our mutual, respectful attentiveness and even more firmly dedicated to our mutual endeavor. On the other hand, I would rebel—inwardly and probably undetected—in those classrooms where obedience was a one-way street and there was no sense of the collegiality of teacher and learner. I lament those times, which were fortunately rare. What might have been a challenging voyage of discovery became a matter of meeting requirements and deadlines, passing exams, and cranking out papers.

❖ Living into Stability

The vow of stability is more appealing; I suspect all of us yearn for it, consciously or unconsciously, in our highly mobile society. Very few of us, even the relatively young, have lived in the same house all our lives. We may have fixed addresses, but there is always something provisional about them. As people of our time and place, we are on the move—in ways great and small. But Benedict is firm, indeed unshakable in the primacy that he ascribes to the vow of stability *(stabilitas)*. He writes with unusual harshness—especially considering the moderation and encompassing compassion of his Rule—when he speaks of those who do not conform to his standard of stability, those who profess to be monks yet wander about doing as they please.

But as Anthony Bloom, a twentieth-century physician and Orthodox monk, makes clear, stability is for all of us, not only monks:

> You will find stability at the moment when you discover that God is everywhere, that you do not need to seek Him elsewhere, that He is here, and if you do not find Him here it is useless to go and search for Him elsewhere because it is not Him [sic] that is absent from us, it is we who are absent from Him.[4]

Benedictine stability involves a commitment to situation and to persons, which is not the same as narrow enclosure that shuts out the world. We too can experience a Benedictine stability, even as we live amid the changes and the chances of the world. This calls for perseverance, for holding on and hanging in, for making thoughtful choices and staying with them. Here we may face a harder task than many of Benedict's monks, for we are inundated with choices and possibilities, even for "good" and "important" things—charities, causes, spiritual disciplines. Even on an ordinary day I sometimes feel like an overindulged child on Christmas morning: should I listen to Taizé chant or a Schubert Mass while I labor at the computer? Should I have cereal or a bagel for breakfast? Should I wear my blue suit or the black one? Everything I own seems to be either black or blue, but still decisions must be made. When the day's work is done, will I read that fascinating biography or turn my brain off as I immerse myself in a whodunit?

What might stability look like for today's ordinary, on-the-go seeker? It might mean returning to the church even when you feel it has run off the rails, when the old rules of your childhood have disappeared along with the "Thee's" and "Thou's." Or it might mean remaining committed to a congregation that seems hopelessly wrong-headed, where everyone is significantly older or younger than you, where children either run rampant or are firmly squelched, where the wrong people are consistently elected to the vestry, where worship is too informal or too stuffy, where you sing and clap to South African marching tunes when you are yearning for Anglican chant. Commitment to *stabilitas* demands that we at least give present circumstances a good try before we move on to the greener pasture down the street. Quite probably it too will disappoint, perhaps in new and different ways that we could never have imagined.

Living into stability might mean sticking to a job after it has lost its glamour. I realized this in my days as a classroom teacher. Preparation of a new course was always exciting—and a terrible amount of work. I would read more books than I could ever pack into a semester's presentations, carefully structure the syllabus, and plan the lectures. The first time I offered the course was a challenge: despair when a day's lecture did not have the impact I had hoped, and exhilaration when one hit the bull's-eye. The second go-round would be more comfortable, but would still have its demanding, uncertain moments. Yet by the time my lecture notes became dog-eared, with marginal notes in assorted colors, the course—for me—was no longer an adventure but one more exercise in stability. The students appeared to be happy: either I had managed to summon a degree of contagious enthusiasm in the classroom or they were extraordinarily polite young people. Or maybe the course wasn't all that bad; perhaps it had even deepened with repetition.

Learning a new language, acquiring even minimal mastery of a musical instrument, facing the daunting task of dealing with a new computer program (at least for me!)—all call for us to submit to that stern teacher *stabilitas.* There are no shortcuts: it is a matter of hanging in and moving on step by step. For that matter, stability, like obedience, is a component in the glue that holds a marriage together. I remember the excitement of preparing the very first meals for my brand-new husband. Now, nearly fifty years later—how many meals would that add up to?—I still enjoy time in the kitchen, but I can scarcely call it exciting. He probably feels the same way about a lot of things that I haven't even noticed, including the menus.

If by traveling the road of mutual obedience we are "going to God," stability is essential for the journey. It is one of the basic assumptions of our faith that God is to be encountered where one is at any given moment. No matter how often we might change our physical dwelling place, it is essential to be spiritually stable and centered. In escaping the confusion and dissonance of a society that offers us too much of everything, both good and bad, helpful and harmful, we are anchored instead of drifting aimlessly.

❖ *Conversion of Life*
Completing and complementing the work of stability is the third Benedictine vow of *conversatio morum,* translated variously as "reformation of life" or "fidelity to the monastic life."[5] This vow of fidelity is really a commitment to ongoing conversion. If life under the Rule is not static, but a journey to God, the vow of *conversatio morum* is the dedication of self to change. It may be difficult to see that new life is coming, that our letting go and the redirecting of ourselves is movement toward new life, and that our loss is only apparent—or at least outweighed by our gain.

Not long ago I spent a day going through a big box of old family photographs. It was rather like an archaeological dig: I saw myself as a chubby, determined-looking child; a quite pretty blonde college student (this surprised me—at the time I could see only my deficiencies); a responsible-looking young matron; an academic decked out in full regalia of cap, gown, and hood; a priest in a neat black suit and stiff white collar; and—finally—a slightly shopworn grandmother. Once I got past my surprise at the way my body had changed, imperceptibly but inexorably, over the years, I was struck by all the changes, internal and external, that marked my path. Some of its twists and turns had not been chosen; they marked the natural progress from childhood to maturity. But others were the result of conscious decisions: to pull up my roots and move a half-continent away from home to immerse myself in graduate school, to marry, to abandon a promising academic career to be a stay-at-home mother, and most recently to devote the final decades of my life to the ordained ministry.

One might see these times of redirection as "career changes," but in fact they mark something deeper. When I was young, I could not have articulated what motivated me. I simply knew that there was always "more"—not money, prestige, or power, but an indefinable something more. Parallel to the outer changes were inner changes, almost imperceptible at the time but recognizable to me in retrospect. Each carried with it some loss: one can't after all have everything or, literally or spiritually, be in two places at once. Each brought with it a growth in self-knowledge. Only in maturity did I come across an insight from the fourteenth-century holy woman Julian of Norwich. Astute psychologist as she was, she realized that the soul could not know God until it knew its own self, nor could it know itself until it knew God. In that sense, my own life has been a series of big and little conversions, although nothing so dramatic as Christian-hating Saul's being knocked to the ground, blinded, and turned into Paul, the missionary. At least not yet.

Rather, at each turning point, my understanding of God has grown and changed. The stern but just God of my childhood prayers has turned out to have other aspects that were never part of our Sunday school curriculum. That Jesus is called Teacher more than forty times in the gospels implies that teaching can be a holy calling, that the relationship of teacher to student is—or should be—a sacred one. The experience of giving birth is as close as I have come to being present at creation. The times of helplessness that are inevitable if we let ourselves love deeply, especially if the loved ones are our children, mirror in a small way the watch at the foot of the cross. Theological study demanded that I put my brain to work when it would be easy to stay in a place of fuzzy piety. Finally, the irrevocable fact of aging brings home daily the reality of diminishment and mortality. A lifetime of turning and turning and turning again, which is what conversion means, has bit by bit destroyed my bland, two-dimensional images of God and replaced them with a multifaceted Mystery. Something tells me that I am not done yet. *Conversatio morum* is the work of a lifetime.

❖ *The Freedom of Poverty*
The traditional monastic vow of poverty is implicit in the linking of stability with the work of ongoing conversion, which demands openness and detachment in its insistence that all things be held lightly. I find it much easier to romanticize poverty than to experience it. Certainly, it would never occur to me to seek it out and embrace it. I find it hard to imagine how stark, unmitigated poverty, where someone must struggle to survive at subsistence level, could nourish spiritual growth.

Some kinds of poverty are freely chosen—or, if poverty is imposed on us, we may summon sufficient strength and grace to embrace it. In accepting this poverty, which is a condition and constant reminder of our human smallness, we can afford to hold all things loosely because we accept our limitation. Moreover, we are assured that despite our anxieties and tendency to hoard, there will be enough. So

Jesus reminds his friends not to worry about what they will eat or wear—will it be caviar or peanut butter, raw silk or polyester? It doesn't really matter; don't worry. There will be enough. Worry, especially about things that ultimately do not matter, is an ugly little false god. Give him an inch, and he will take over, fill up all the space, and look around for more. When we embrace the kind of poverty taught by Jesus, we are accepting our nothingness in the grand scheme of things. We know that we are transient: we came into this world naked, and we will depart without anything—despite the debts our loved ones might accrue by giving us a grand send-off.

In his Rule Benedict does not speak of poverty *per se*. Rather, his monks are permitted to own nothing as individuals. There is assurance of sufficiency of food, clothing, and shelter, but all goods are held in common. This radical letting-go of personal possessions is a reminder that indeed all is gift and that ownership is illusory. Even as I sit writing in a house fully paid for, in a room filled with a lifetime's accumulation of books and furniture, I know that Benedict and his fellow monastics were right: I really own nothing. All is gift, and ultimately nothing is really ours. Voluntary poverty, dangerously countercultural, could be a path to inner freedom if we can embrace it, willingly and totally. I'm still working on it.

Sitting on the mountainside, Jesus told his friends, "Blessed are the poor in spirit, for theirs is the kingdom of heaven." I think that he was talking about letting go of all those things—tangible and intangible—that divert and distract us, that keep us from God. If we let ourselves become poor in spirit, we are not so much impoverished as blessedly simplified. The extraneous is stripped away, and we become spiritually agile and alive. We hold everything with an open hand because we know that ultimately it isn't worth very much after all. We can let go of the compulsion always to need just a little bit more. This very human urge reminds me of my dachshund of blessed memory: she always wanted to walk eighteen inches beyond the extent of her leash. Granted her wish, she then realized that the really good stuff was just a few inches farther on. We should know better; we should live in the assurance that there is enough.

❖ *Living Temperately in Our Bodies*
While I was researching "chastity" on the Internet, I came across a site inviting me to explore chastity belts. It was clear from the titillating come-on, even to my naive and unpracticed eye, that this site was not going to augment my scholarly knowledge of oppressive medieval marriage practices. Just as it is time to reclaim a healthy asceticism, it is time to reclaim chastity, which relates primarily to sexual behavior. For monastics, this means preservation of a virgin or widowed state, so that all power of the body and soul may be devoted to the service of God. In one of the old movies that enlivened my ultra-Protestant younger days, a radiant Audrey Hepburn entered the chapel in a traditional wedding dress, to be exchanged for an austere habit at a crucial point in the ceremony. It put her out of the running as a bride for anybody but God. For the single person, celibacy means abstinence, and for the married and those in committed partnerships, it means fidelity.

The true meaning of chastity, however, goes much deeper. It is certainly more than abstaining from sexual activity. In one of his very few teachings on sexual behavior, Jesus says, "You have heard that it was said, 'You shall not commit adultery.' But I say to you that everyone who looks at a woman with lust has already committed adultery with her in his heart" (Matthew 5:27–28). The Greek word here is *porneia,* possibly a general term referring to sins of the flesh. Jesus is not dealing with an outward offense, but with the origin of these actions. Truck drivers do not whistle at me anymore, nor do construction workers assess my physical charms when I pass by a building site, but I can remember when they did. Far from feeling complimented, I felt sullied by their attention. What a pity that Jesus wasn't on the spot to set them right. They were probably not motivated by serious lust, but it was lust nonetheless. There is no specific vow of chastity in Benedict's Rule, but its observance is implicit. Augustine, on the other hand, is unusually explicit in his Rule:

> Even if your gaze happens to fall on a woman you should not stare at her.... You cannot claim to have pure minds if you have impure eyes, for an impure eye is the messenger of an impure heart. When impure hearts exchange messages by their glances, even though the tongue remains silent,... then chastity takes flight from their behavior even though there has been no despoiling of the body. (chp. IV)

Like Jesus, Augustine is as much concerned with motivation, with unacted-upon impulses and preoccupations, as with overt actions.

Every now and then I find it illuminating to poke around in the corners of the *Book of Common Prayer* that I do not regularly visit. The catechism is one such corner, tucked away at the very end. There is quite a lot of wisdom and good plain information in this series of questions and answers. When asked, "What is our duty toward our neighbor?" the correct response is a summary of the Ten Commandments. Rather than disavowing adultery directly, the response deals more broadly and deeply with chastity: it is our duty toward our neighbor to keep the body "in temperance, soberness and chastity." The response to the same question in the contemporary is more succinct: "To use all our bodily desires as God intended" (BCP, 848). Chastity is still primarily concerned with sexual behavior but can encompass other sorts of destructive self-indulgence: overindulgence in food, drink, nicotine, and questionable sites on the World Wide Web—to name just a few. Ultimately, if we live chastely, we show our love for our neighbors by our reverence for them. The commitment to living temperately and soberly might sound like embracing a particularly grim and perpetual Lent, but it really means living in awareness and valuing our embodiment.

Benedict calls his Rule "the way to God," not an end in itself but a helpful guide for the journey. Surely it can be no coincidence that the book of Acts tells us one of the earliest names for Christianity was the Way. That Way was followed by ordinary people, people with families, friends, maybe even enemies, people who worked hard and had many of the same worries we have today. People like us. People who, like the child Samuel, had heard their names called in the night. Maybe the call came very faintly, but God had got their attention, and they knew they had to do something about it. To follow the Way is not to wander aimlessly, but to observe the rules of the road.

part 2

The Essentials

3

Cultivating the Vines

The ancient monastic rules provide us with useful models for structuring our lives, but we need to remember that Augustine and Benedict were writing for celibates living relatively focused lives in strictly regulated communities, so their Rules have limitations when it comes to how "the rest of us" might live out the vows of obedience, stability, and conversion of life. Like our medieval brothers and sisters in the monastery or the village, we are gay and straight; married, partnered, or single; young and old; we have jobs that we love and jobs that deaden our souls; we yearn for meaningful work, or we yearn for more free time to do the things we love. Yet in contrast to our early medieval brothers and sisters, we are inundated with choices and possibilities that would have been unthinkable even for the privileged in the fifth and sixth centuries. If we are to be good stewards of our abundance of time, energy, and creativity, we need to live in awareness. We need a rule, not to hem us in but to enable us to flourish.

Before we can formulate a wise rule for our lives, we need to take a hard look at ourselves and ask, "What is the shape of my life right now? What does my stewardship of time, energy, substance, and creativity look like? What have

I been missing? What are my areas of disproportion? Am I oppressed, or do I—despite outer circumstances—live in inner freedom?" If we are honest, this exercise in self-examination can be as alarming and painfully illuminating as keeping track of calories in a food journal. Most of us have done some version of this. A breakfast of Special K with skim milk, half a grapefruit, and black coffee—and then there was that doughnut at the ten o'clock coffee break. Back to the program for lunch: water-packed tuna, lettuce, and an apple. But then there was the plate of cookies that somebody left in the staff kitchen; they were small and no one was looking, so two disappeared in a heartbeat. And so on through the day—a Spartan dinner to make up for earlier lapses, but somehow a bag of chips—not a terribly big bag, of course—disappeared during a late rerun of *Law and Order.* Not happy with ourselves and not particularly well nourished, we go to bed vowing to do better tomorrow.

Carefully keeping track of our time can reveal the same kind of mindless lapses, wasteful living that brings no real joy or profit. This is by no means the same as the enjoyment of restorative leisure time or the inevitable fallow times that are necessary to the creative process. Rather, it is a matter of failing to live in awareness of the preciousness of each day. I have known folk who adhere to meticulous budgets regarding their expenditure of money but who are quite unconscious of their expenditure of time. They finish a crowded day and wonder where on earth the hours have gone. To be sure, tasks great and small have been accomplished, and the requirements of the job have been met. But a review of a typical day's activities would not stand up well to the principle of living every day as if it were your last.

Our use, abuse, or enjoyment of time is the raw material not only of our days, but of crafting a rule of life. Time is a gift from God. The span of our years may vary, but each day we have the same amount: 24 hours, 1440 minutes.

That day will not come again. Yet as we become ever more obsessed with time, we seem to have less. We are overworked and tightly scheduled, paddling along frantically with our noses just above the water line. The unceasing busyness of our high-achieving corner of the world can leave us with no time for prayer, let alone a few uncluttered moments of reflection. We crowd out God along with our joy and spontaneity. Relentless busyness, which is one aspect of the sin of sloth, can dry up our souls. It took me a long time to figure this out. My idea of sloth—if I thought of it at all—was the pleasant torpor of a lazy summer day, lying in the hammock and reading very disposable fiction. That can be extremely pleasant, but I kept forgetting that God did not suggest but *command* that we stop, rest, and observe the Sabbath. All the pressures, commitments, and obligations will be right where we left them when we return, but the temporary suspension of work will help restore them to correct proportions.

I wish that I had a dollar—in less inflated times I have wished for a quarter—for every time someone sitting in my quiet little room at the church has said, "I don't have time to pray." I have no business looking shocked because I have said the same thing too many times myself. Upon reflection, I realize that my friends and I are not really concerned with carving out ten, twenty, or thirty minutes from our day for an intentional time of prayer. Instead, it is a matter of choices and priorities. Since we manage to get almost everything else done in the course of twenty-four hours, I am convinced that the problem goes deeper. Even as we march purposefully upward and onward, inwardly we are adrift. It is not a more rigorous schedule that we need. Rather, we need to establish our priorities. Where, after all, does prayer fit in the day? Ahead or behind returning phone calls or loading the dishwasher? Ahead or behind the obligatory twenty minutes on the exercise bicycle or trip to the gym? We did not come into this world equipped with a spiritual road map or an owner's manual, so we need to write our own.

The following chapters of this book are intended to do just that. Each one discusses one distinctive aspect of our lives—our families, our solitude, our creativity, our money, our fear of abundance, our friends and enemies, our prayer, our use of power—that is essential to who we are and how we are going to live with each other and with God. Each chapter is followed by some reflection questions. The creation of a rule of life can be a stimulating exercise because it compels us to reflect candidly on our stewardship of our time, energy, and our very selves. It compels us to ask: do I take God seriously, as the foundation of all that I believe, do, and am? It reminds us of the preciousness of each day, of the ordinary that is so easy to take for granted. When Benedict instructs his monks to treat everyday utensils as if they were sacred vessels on the altar, it is as if he were saying, "Pay attention! Take nothing for granted." The hours and minutes of your days are the same.

4

Under One Roof

❖❖ On those days when the world is too much with me and the people in my life want too much from me, I think that I would enjoy being a hermit. I know that in those times when I have lived in solitude—on sabbatical in Jenkins Hollow or on long trips by myself with no obligations to anyone else—I can be remarkably free of small sins and peccadilloes. I am not rude or impatient. I am serene because there is no one, even—or especially—a loved one, to irritate me. I am not selfish, probably because there is no need to share anything with anybody. With great stretches of uninterrupted time I am quite faithful about saying my prayers. It can indeed be delightful to play at being a holy hermit, especially when the food is good and the bed is comfortable.

But we know that, right from the beginning, we are stuck with one another. We are meant to be together in families, households, or communities of some sort. As Genesis 2 has it, Adam was living a carefree bachelor's existence in the Garden of Eden. He wasn't complaining, but the LORD God decided that he needed companionship or maybe a challenge: "It is not good that the man should be alone; I will make him a helper to be his partner." So God created all the animals and invited Adam to name them.

None filled the bill, although some probably came closer than others—I would choose an intelligent, friendly dog over a raccoon or skunk any day—so then, in the version of the story that makes good feminists bristle, woman was created from Adam's rib. That is how it all began: all the pain and wonder, the complexity and joy of people living together. And the rest is history.

We human beings are impelled to cluster together and to try to stay together, not just to reproduce ourselves but to love and support one another, to be faithful and forgiving. I think about this at weddings, when a new family has been created, and I can't help wondering: *Do they have any idea what they are getting into? Maybe it's better that they don't know.* I think about our innate need for connection at funerals, too, when we mark a break in the chain that has held a family together. It makes me marvel at the enduring power of love that has kept often unlikely and unlovely people knit together for years, for decades. It is easy to forget the heroism of day-in, day-out living together. We need our helpers and our partners—in our marriages, in our traditional or not-so-traditional households, in our communities whatever form they might take.

❖ *What is a Family?*
Families have been troubled or at least challenged since Cain slew Abel, but each generation has its own flavor. Late at night when I am surfing the channels, I often come across the family sitcoms of past decades. Stay-at-home mothers, immaculately groomed, might let themselves be mildly exasperated by the antics of their children or (slightly dim) husbands, but they were never impatient or angry. Children worked hard at pleasing their parents and, should they commit some minor infraction of the household code, were contrite. Fathers exercised their authority with benevolent firmness. Their work, whatever it was, did not consume them: they came home on time to sit down at the family dinner table. It is a world that never was, yet

we are still sure that somewhere out there life under the family roof runs smoothly, that children never disappoint, and that parents are paragons.

Our secular spirituality has come to idealize the nuclear family, even as sociologists tell us that the number of one-parent households is increasing dramatically and that the number of one-person households even more so. We are yearning for kinship and homesick for home, the warm and untidy home of extended and often tangled relationships. Some of us are alone—either by choice or by circumstance. Some of us are grieving the physical death of a loved one or the death of a relationship. Some of us live under one roof with the requisite number of spouses, children, and grandchildren, but still find life hard and bleak. Some of us are recovering or perhaps still overcome by an earlier life of neglect or abuse. Some of us are just plain tired.

It is time to let go of the old clichés and rethink what we mean by family. Jesus offers some powerful teaching here in a story told in Matthew, Mark, and Luke. As he teaches, surrounded by a crowd of friends and followers, his mother, brothers, and sisters come and stand outside, calling to him. Jesus refuses to join them: "Here are my mother and my brothers!" he tells the crowd. "Whoever does the will of God is my brother and sister and mother" (Mark 3:31–35; see also Matthew 12:46–50 and Luke 8:19–21). On the surface this is harsh treatment, yet it can also be seen as an invitation to enlarge the circle and to extend our vision of kinship beyond the biological family. There is room for everyone in that crowd around Jesus.

I experienced this recently when I was teaching in Hong Kong. All my students were Chinese and all much younger than I. It was a joy to be with them: we spent long hours in the classroom, we worshiped together, we sang Taizé chants in English, Latin, and Cantonese. When it was time for us to part, as we gathered for a group photograph, they told me, "You are our grandmother." I'm not sure how I would have reacted if a similar scene had taken place in the youth-oriented West, but surrounded by my Chinese Christian friends, I was honored to be their grandmother even though we looked very different, we struggled with two languages, and I was clumsy with my chopsticks.

Anyone who has been married for more than six months and certainly any parent of children from infants to adolescents knows that the vision of a family functioning harmoniously with a happily shared vision of what should be done when and how is an attractive but romantic illusion. Divorced parents, sharing custody of their children, are often building the bicycle as they ride it—how can they create a sense of mutual affection and stability when a home has been broken? Gay and lesbian households have their own special flavor, simultaneously like and unlike their heterosexual neighbors. The yearning for community is strong—not the oppressive "togetherness" so successfully marketed after World War II, but deep and sustaining connection. That connection is elusive; houses seem to be getting bigger, but it often feels as if no one is at home. When my own children were small, every kitchen had a mother in it, watching over the neighborhood young at play in the alley. Our kitchens now are increasingly high-tech, but how do you have a meal when nobody is there to eat it?

The New Testament is not very helpful about family values. Jesus, unmarried at an age when most Jewish men were husbands and fathers, exhibits a cavalier attitude toward families as he gathers his followers around him. Think about the call of the disciples from their wives' point of view: Jesus meets Peter and Andrew, James and John, as they are tending their nets. He says, "Follow me," and immediately they abandon their livelihood without a second thought. They abandon their families as well: did they ever go home to tell their wives that they would not be there for dinner? Did they make any provision for their families? When, in my imagination, I translate this story into the present time, were I the wife of Peter, Andrew, James, or John, I would be furious. "You did *what?* What about the health plan? Your pension? College for the children? Are you planning on coming back sometime? How am I going to manage? Who will look after the children if I have to get a job?" If I were Peter's mother-in-law, who got up and served them after Jesus healed her from an unnamed illness—I always picture her frying chicken in the hot kitchen of my childhood—I would not have been particularly gracious. Grateful as I was for my healing, I might have been tempted to slam his plate down, just a little. Jesus might have been an effective healer, but he also certainly knew how to disrupt a household.

Yet from the cross he teaches us about life under one roof.

> When Jesus saw his mother and the disciple whom he loved standing beside her, he said to his mother, "Woman, here is your son." Then he said to the disciple, "Here is your mother." And from that hour the disciple took her into his own home. (John 19:26–27)

We encounter this new household in first chapter of the Acts of the Apostles. After witnessing the ascension, Jesus' followers return to Jerusalem and go to

> the room upstairs, where they were staying, Peter, and John, and James, and Andrew, Philip and Thomas, Bartholomew and Matthew, James son of Alpheus, and Simon the Zealot, and Judas son of James. All these were constantly devoting themselves to prayer, together with certain women, including Mary the mother of Jesus, as well as his brothers. (Acts 1:13–14)

Who were the "certain women"? Were they the disciples' wives or sisters, or possibly quite independent followers of Jesus? Had they, like their male colleagues, simply walked away from their old lives and responsibilities? Maybe Peter's mother-in-law was there. It is an appealing picture of a multigenerational holy commune, some of whose members were related by blood but all of them united in their faith.

✤ *Living in Community*
The rise of Western monasticism was a radical social innovation, as groups of quite disparate men chose to live celibate lives of prayer in an intentional community, quite unlike the church of the first centuries, the biological family, or the loosely knit communities of the holy eccentrics of the desert. Augustine's monks were men of widely different social backgrounds: poor and affluent, lettered and unlettered. So his concise Rule is concerned, as is Benedict's, with the role and behavior of the individual in the community. Its aim is integration, which my faithful Webster's dictionary tells me means "to form, coordinate, or blend into a functioning or unified whole." Our lives in the complex and overstimulated twenty-first century are very different from those of determined God-seekers of fifth-century Hippo. Yet if we can make the necessary translations, the monastic rules offer some practical help because they are concerned with the details of ordinary life.

Monasteries were not democracies: the abbot was definitely in charge. Yet his authority was to be exercised carefully and prayerfully, the person wielding power never daring to lose sight of the awesome responsibility accompanying it. It is hard work being a parent, caregiver of the frail aged, or head of any household. Indeed, there have been times in my life when—naively perhaps—I would have been happy to change places with an abbot any day. Decisions are to be made so authority must be accepted: a wishy-washy parent can be as destructive as a harsh one, and an erratic, impatient caregiver can be abusive of the helpless. One accepts authority and the power that goes with it, knowing that it is a burden rather than a privilege.

Even a cursory reading of the ancient rules makes clear that the early monastics were, like all the rest of us, a fallible bunch. Augustine cautions his monks to look out for one another when they are in dangerous places, that is, where they might possibly encounter women:

> Therefore when you are in company together in church or elsewhere where women are present, you should protect one another's modesty, for in this way God who dwells within you will protect you from yourselves. (chp. IV)

At first glance, this warning has little to do with our life in community in American society in the twenty-first century, maybe even for today's monks. At a deeper level, however, Augustine's caution is about mutual responsibility. We are indeed our brothers' and sisters' keepers. Hence we need to support one another in awareness of our own human fallibility. We should not be heartened by another's weakness, like the Pharisee who thanked God that, whatever his own shortcomings, he was infinitely superior to the despised tax collector. The Pharisee in me can feel very good after scanning the morning newspaper. I may not be perfect, but I have not murdered anyone nor have I embezzled even so much as a postage stamp from the parish office. Like the Pharisee, I bear no resemblance to the thieves, rogues, adulterers, or crooked civil servants who fill the pages of the *Washington Post*. Yet like it or not, I am their sister, enjoined to love them. Even as I cannot condone their actions—and tax collectors in first-century Palestine were a pretty despicable lot—I dare not lose sight either of their humanity or the dangers of self-satisfaction and complacency. Most importantly, I dare not lose sight that in our common humanity we are not so very different.

Closer to home and probably more to the point, like Augustine's monks we need to look out for one another, to support our neighbors and let ourselves be supported. After years of undignified wrestling for its possession, I am beginning to learn to permit younger friends to carry my suitcase. At the other end of the spectrum, I take delight in my ministry of hanging out with the young mothers of our congregation. They do not want a surrogate mother or grandmother, but they seem to enjoy a good jolt of crone wisdom now and then. Wonderfully, it all averages out: when we are each other's keepers, we both give and receive, and everyone benefits.

Trust lies at the heart of life in community. Augustine instructs his monks that if one of the brothers has a hidden pain and reports it, he is to be believed. Unfortunately, in our own households we start to go wrong when our children are young: "It doesn't hurt *that* much.... Don't cry.... It's just a little bump or scrape or sting." So we learn early to bottle up our feelings, deny our pain, and repress our fears. I doubt that Augustine encouraged his monks to turn into hypochondriacs or slackers, but there is considerable canniness in his compassion. Our defenses drop away when we are believed: we do not have to try so hard, and reasonable proportion is restored. When we feel that we are truly heard, seen, and known, we can afford to let go and be generous.

His endearing name for the monk called *famulus Dei*—a household servant—is revelatory of the structure of the household. Unlike the ménage depicted in the old television series *Upstairs, Downstairs* or Merchant-Ivory films about an Edwardian England that probably never was, everyone in Augustine's community lives "below stairs" in a kind of democracy where every household servant merits credulity.

❖ Broken Communities

One of my favorite monastic faults is murmuring, condemned by both Augustine and Benedict. You do not have to spend long in a typical parish or office or school to know precisely what they were talking about. Outwardly conforming, even impeccable in the performance of all duties, the murmurer spreads little drops of poison all over the place. Benedict's teaching about the equitable distribution of food or clothing sounds familiar to anyone who has ever arbitrated discussions about who got the biggest piece of cake or the corner piece with the most frosting: "Above all, let not the evil of murmuring appear for any reason whatsoever in the least word or sign" (chp. 34). In other words, accept what is allotted to you without a fuss. The arguments over the amount of cake frosting or who gets the last cookie are eventually outgrown (usually!), but the evil of murmuring is alive and well.

Probably all of us can confess that we have been guilty of murmuring at times—after all, murmuring is, in a grim sort of way, rather pleasant. The typical murmurer in a twenty-first-century parish, office, school, or neighborhood association can see everything that is wrong with the present management. The murmurer could certainly do a better job than his supervisor, the rector, or the chairman of the education committee—but God forbid that the murmurer should stand up and say so! Confrontation, which is not necessarily hostile but can be helpful truth spoken in love, seems too difficult and risky. After all, the murmurer might be wrong. Or compelled to move off the sidelines and *do* something. Maybe even to *change*. It is infinitely easier to lurk around the edges and luxuriate in hurt feelings, carefully nursed slights, and just plain grumpiness.

Excommunication was a severe monastic punishment for obstinacy, disobedience, pride, or murmuring. This meant exclusion from the refectory and from full participation in worship. In other words, no longer able to eat or pray with his brothers, the offender was effectively removed from the community, even though still physically present. Excommunication nowadays is an equally drastic step but, to my knowledge, is rarely applied. At least our common garden-variety murmurers are spared, for, according to the rubrics, you have to be living a "notoriously evil life" or completely unrepentant of major wrongdoing before, after due warning, you are denied communion (BCP, 409). This is the stuff of drama, though not necessarily high drama but the B-movie of the 1940s. If there are notorious sinners in our congregations, they are rarely identified, at least not publicly, and little internecine feuds manage to flourish quietly. Community can be broken even if everyone continues to come to the communion rail. Wittingly or unwittingly, we can exclude and close out the misfits and the undesirables. We comfortably assume that the days of blatant racial segregation in the Christian community are past—but are they really? Even more prevalent, though, is tacit excommunication on socioeconomic lines. The appearance of the disheveled or disoriented in our well-groomed congregations causes unease, even if we give no overt sign of our discomfort. The broader community also has its own unwritten rules of excommunication. Crudely anti-Semitic remarks and jokes of the sort that were common when I was growing up are no longer heard, at least not in the circles I frequent. But I suspect that too often cold-heartedness and contempt toward all those whom we would push to the margins have just gone underground. I can't remember in which novel Iris Murdoch wisely says, "Everyone excludes someone." God, I am convinced, has no margins. We create them and then populate them with the excommunicated: women, Muslims, gay and lesbian folk, liberals, conservatives, Republicans, Democrats, the aged, and the obese. And sometimes we excommunicate ourselves. Life is certainly less complicated if we do not have to deal with the untidiness of real life together.

❖ *Sharing Space, Sharing Lives*
In the course of a lifetime we live under multiple roofs. Sharing space with a roommate is just as complex and often as frustrating and difficult as life together in the nuclear family. The neatnik and the slob, the smoker and nonsmoker, the studious and the social butterfly are often thrown together in those situations where strangers are expected to live in harmony. I understand that college

admissions officers perform remarkable feats on their computers to assure at least some compatibility when assigning roommates, but that first sharing of limited space must be a shock for the privileged young who are accustomed to having their own rooms to decorate or desecrate as they please. The memories of my own early days in a crowded dorm are still vivid. I was probably a terrible roommate, being compulsively neat and given to long hours of silent study. At the time, I was sure that all the fault lay with my fellow resident. By my senior year, though, I had teamed up with a pre-med student who was even more compulsive than I. We got along fine.

Life in the workplace is also life under one roof. We bump up against one another, we irritate one another, and we support one another—sometimes all in the same day. It is surely no accident that the psychological principles of family systems have been applied so successfully to the dynamics of the workplace. If nothing else, they remind us that we are not isolated people performing our own tasks, but that, for good or ill, we are interconnected in very human ways like biological families. Or, for that matter, like Benedict's monks.

When I am able to see my colleagues in this light, not sentimentally like the families extolled in greeting cards but as complicated human beings who are both like me and unlike me, I am enriched. We live together under rules spoken but more usually unspoken. As in a biological family we know each other's strengths and fallibilities. I know that one of my colleagues always wants that desirable corner piece of the cake at a staff birthday party. I know that another can always be counted on to pick up the slack if someone falls short. I know who always arrives barely on time or maybe even late, and who is on hand five minutes early. They know the same sort of thing about me. For many hours of the week we live under one roof together. There may be bumpy places, but I cannot imagine working any other way. I have to wonder what it would be like to sit alone all day in a tollbooth on a bridge or freeway. It must be lonely to be all alone under that little roof. Those of us who live alone, whether by choice or circumstances, risk isolation. They are surely more comfortable than my person in the cramped tollbooth, but are nevertheless deprived of the rich messiness (or the messy richness) of daily life under one roof with others. Sometimes, when life gets a little too crowded, I am tempted to envy these folk. Yet, for the long pull, we need each other—back to the story of Adam in the garden. It did not take long for our forebears to be driven out of Eden. I think they just outgrew it and needed a real challenge. In any event, those who live alone are faced with a choice: they can opt for isolation, or they can find temporary but genuine shelter under other roofs—the workplace, the parish, the school, wherever they find the meaningful company of others.

❖ *Receiving the Guest*
People who know nothing else of Benedictine ethos are usually familiar with the call to let all guests who arrive at the gates of the monastery be received like Christ. Benedict might well have been paraphrasing the letter to the Hebrews: we never know with whom we are dealing—angels or Jesus traveling among us incognito. One of the outreach efforts in the parish where I serve is the Water Ministry. Four days a week the homeless—mostly men— come together to wash their clothes, have a shower, and share lunch. These are people who do not "fit" in our well-groomed neighborhood and would look out of place in the nave at eleven o'clock Eucharist on Sunday morning. Their life on the street is bleak and dangerous. Some are crippled by mental illness and addiction. In short, these are society's throwaway people. But for a few hours each week they are under one roof. It is a safe place and a respite, not enough but a tiny bit of transformation nevertheless.

Those guests who sought monastic hospitality in the Middle Ages were all sorts and conditions of people, just as the friends and strangers whom we encounter run the gamut of humanity. So we greet archbishops and sidewalk panhandlers in the same spirit: grumpy clerks at the supermarket and a welcome visitor, the rude person at the motor vehicles office and the florist's delivery man who brings three dozen roses, the child who interrupts a few precious moments of quiet and the telephone caller who tells me that I have won the lottery. It is always a good idea to act as if we were entertaining angels—just in case. If we took just this one bit of the Rule to heart, we could transform the world. I confess, though, that while I manage fairly well a good deal of the time, I have not yet been able to receive telephone solicitors, especially the ones who call when I am up to my elbows in dinner preparation, as if they were Christ himself. But then, we are all works in progress.

To stick it out under one roof—whether in a decades-long marriage, a complex and sometimes difficult workplace, or even for a few hours of hospitality in the Water Ministry—demands a commitment to that ancient Benedictine virtue, stability. This means, to some extent, putting ourselves aside while at the same time accepting responsibility and accountability. It means putting up with tedium, disappointment, and occasional conflict. It means just showing up, even on the days when we would rather be somewhere else. Living into stability is slow work, and its fruits are not immediately apparent. It reminds me of an old, old television commercial for a laundry detergent promising to rid the wearer of "ring around the collar." How did you know you had it? The point is: you didn't, until other people gasped and pointed at you. The fruits of stability are like that: we don't even notice them, but others do.

✌︎✦︎✌︎

Questions for Prayer and Pondering

❖   In many of our buildings we have installed devices to detect gases such as radon that might otherwise poison the atmosphere with deadly effect. How effective is your murmur detector? Do its batteries need recharging? Remember: Benedict did not dub murmuring "evil" for nothing.

❖   Whom have you excommunicated? To paraphrase Iris Murdoch: everybody excommunicates somebody. How can you accept and welcome their presence as part of the *koinonia* of the Holy Spirit?

❖   Do you feel yourself excommunicated? How can you claim or reclaim your place in the family?

❖   Read the Baptismal Covenant starting on page 304 in the Episcopal Church's *Book of Common Prayer* as if it were your rule for living with everyone around you. As you linger on each question, ponder how your response might manifest itself specifically in your everyday life.

5

Both Host and Guest

A memory of hospitality: It was 1951 and I was a young, naive student backpacking in Europe with my good friend Ardyth during our long spring break at a Swiss university. We were riding through Spain on a third-class train—a form of conveyance, I suspect, that no longer exists. Third-class compartments accommodated five people on each side, tightly packed on facing wooden benches, just a step up from a freight car. There were few tourists then in war-ravaged Europe, even fewer in Franco's Spain, and we were exotic creatures in that little group of country people. No one attempted conversation, but at midday our fellow passengers produced food from their bags and, before they began to eat, solemnly offered to share with us. We were impressed by the men's knives slicing the bread and salami—long and sharp, honed to razor thinness. Only after we had declined and showed them our two oranges did they begin to eat. Later, despite the discomfort of the hard bench, I fell asleep. I woke with a start, sensing someone near me, and opened my eyes to see a grizzled old man tenderly covering me with my own coat that had slipped to the floor. He was the same man who had offered us food earlier; he might have been my grandfather. I settled down for a good nap, knowing that I was enfolded in care.

Even now I can close my eyes, see the stark cramped space, feel the hard wood, see the wrinkled face with its stubble of white beard. He wasn't smiling, but he looked kind. He knew that he would never see me again, but he was offering hospitality to this strange young creature who had wandered into his world. There was something impersonal yet intimate and almost primitive in our silent interaction. It reminds me of stories of nomadic life, where hospitality was a necessity. Since the traveler never knew when he might require hospitality himself, welcoming the stranger was not so much an act of generosity as of insurance against the future. Guests were to be treated with respect, offered food for themselves and their animals, and given water to wash off dusty feet. Even an enemy enjoyed protection for three days; and after his departure from the host's tent, he was safe from attack for thirty-six hours after eating, which was presumed to be the time he would be sustained by the food provided by his host.

My meanderings through the dictionary, a favorite activity during attacks of procrastination, have taught me about the complex and unsentimental nature of our care for the stranger: the words "host," "guest," "hostile," "hostage," "hospital," and "hospitality" all spring from the same Latin root *hostis,* meaning stranger or enemy. To extend hospitality means widening the circle temporarily, perhaps taking a risk. Our generosity may be rejected, and we certainly dare not hope for thanks or reimbursement. To offer hospitality is an obligation. There is nothing soft or mushy about it. It has nothing to do with artificial standards of behavior.

Yet all too often "hospitality" conjures up, at least for me, images from my youth at the movies: lavish dinner parties that are impeccably served, and receptions filled with elegantly dressed people sipping champagne at Merchant-Ivory house parties. I remember, too, my zealous combing

of Emily Post's *Etiquette,* absorbing the fine points of entertaining that would never have been needed in the Kansas
City of my childhood. (For example, it was considered bad
form for the butler to sport a mustache, a bit of knowledge
that has not yet proved useful.) Yet true hospitality goes
beyond rules and regulations; sometimes it even demands
that rules be broken or at least stretched. True hospitality
demands attentiveness, not so much paying attention to the
placement of the cutlery on the dinner table, but attentiveness and openness to the *other* who has entered our tent.
This means putting ourselves aside at least temporarily, and
suspending judgment as we accept that other as neighbor
and kin.

❖ *God in Disguise*
Jesus makes it clear that the roles of guest and host are inter-
changeable and that we never know to whom we might be
offering hospitality. He has a way of appearing as a guest
and then taking over as host, most notably in the houses of
Simon the Pharisee and Zacchaeus. Simon at least invited
him to dinner, but when Jesus saw Zacchaeus up in the
sycamore tree, he simply invited himself: "Zacchaeus, hurry
and come down; for I must stay at your house today." Only
as an adult did I begin to understand the German table
blessing I had learned as a child: "Come, Lord Jesus, be our
guest, and bless everything that you have given us." We
invite him, only to discover that we are not in charge; and
sometimes he turns up without an invitation. Simon and
Zacchaeus knew, at least in part, who had come to partake
of their hospitality. In the parable of the Last Judgment,
however, Jesus reminds us that he, in the best tradition of
folklore, is the king who comes among his followers incognito. Like the simple folk of old-time radio, who never
managed to recognize the Lone Ranger, those about to be
shunted off among the deficient goats protest: "Lord, when
was it that we saw you hungry or thirsty or a stranger or
naked or sick or in prison, and did not take care of you?"

We are still making the same mistake: failing to recognize him when he turns up on the street or in the bus station or maybe even in our own congregation, especially when he doesn't oblige us by dressing like his pictures.

St. Benedict knew this, and awareness of the God who moves among his people in disguise lies at the heart of his Rule: "Let all guests who arrive be received like Christ, for He is going to say, 'I came as a guest, and you received me'" (chp. 53). He goes on to describe how the guest must be treated: greeted with a deep bow or prostration upon arrival and departure. To be sure, this was a sign of honor to the guest, but more importantly it was an act of adoration of Christ. If necessary, without acknowledging that the obligations of hospitality demanded that he depart from his usual practice, the superior would break his fast to eat with the guest. This was a genuine sacrifice, though not so extreme as the behavior of the desert father Abba Macarius, who ate and drank with his hosts as an act of gratitude for their hospitality, then deprived himself even more drastically of food and water as an act of penance. His brothers eventually learned not to offer him anything at all.

Hospitality in the Hebrew Scriptures grows directly from the nomadic tradition. Hence Abraham's generous, almost obsequious reception of the three strangers under the oaks of Mamre is merely correct, not excessive. At least initially, he has no idea that he is welcoming the messengers of the LORD, if not the LORD himself. Similarly, Rebekah's reception of Abraham's servant at the well is no more than to be expected. When he asks for a drink for himself, she obliges and then offers to draw water for all his camels. I have never watered *one* thirsty camel; this must have been a backbreaking undertaking. If Rebekah followed one of the cardinal rules of hospitality, she kept smiling and made it look easy.

Back when I was still a Presbyterian, wary of popish practices, I visited a college friend who was a novice in an Anglican religious order. When I walked onto the grounds,

I had entered a whole new world! Charlotte—now Sister Michael—was waiting for me at the gate. Instead of going off to chat in the garden, she took me straight to the guest mistress. Sister Benedicta, a stately woman right out of central casting, greeted me with not one but two kisses. (Continental style, although I didn't realize it at the time.) *This woman doesn't even know me,* I thought, *but she's certainly friendly.* Long after, I realized that I had been greeted with the ritual kiss of peace, welcomed as a sojourning guest if only for a couple of hours on a hot Sunday afternoon. Then she insisted that we sit down for brownies and a glass of milk. Later on, when I became a fairly frequent Sunday afternoon visitor at the convent, I was always greeted warmly, always with the ritual kiss, sometimes but not always with a plate of cookies. It began to feel quite ordinary and predictable. But I have never forgotten that initial visit as a stranger who had dropped in out of nowhere (although actually I had come on a streetcar). I might have been a visitor motivated by curiosity or maybe by a desire to persuade my friend to flee the confinement of this strangely medieval place; or I might have been a prospective novice, carefully dipping my toe into the mysterious pond of the religious life. In any case, it was obvious just to see me, poor graduate student that I was, that I was not a likely financial benefactor to the order. None of this mattered. I was a stranger at the gate and I was received as a welcome guest.

I have tried to remember the spirit of that first meeting with Sister Benedicta at those times when it is important to put myself aside and welcome the stranger, even when I would rather not. She might have been looking forward to a leisurely afternoon off-duty, perhaps mending her socks or taking a nap, or even reading a novel. Whatever her plans for that Sunday afternoon might have been, she left me with the feeling that my arrival at the convent was the best and most important thing that had happened all day.

To receive invited guests at a meal planned for the occasion or to welcome an expected overnight visitor calls for us to put ourselves aside, at least temporarily, and to make a space for them, to enlarge our domestic circle. We offer this kind of hospitality willingly, at least most of the time. It is pleasurable to imagine what food might be appealing, to consider what new book or recent copy of *The New Yorker* we can leave in the guest room, to make sure that the bedside reading light has an adequate bulb, and to check that the guestroom closet is not jammed with our own out-of-season clothes. There are other occasions of hospitality, however, that are more demanding. These are the ones that I try to avoid, especially when I am feeling overextended and crotchety: the urgent phone call from someone I find unreasonably demanding, just when I am running out the door; the impromptu pastoral conversation on a day when I could use some sympathy myself; the unwanted interruption of work or study or solitude under almost all circumstances. Then, too, not all the visitors to our inner space come from outside. We do not often think of offering hospitality to those under our own roof, but a generous response to family interruptions is an act of true hospitality. Our patience can wear very thin, whether we are responding to the persistent queries and petitions of a toddler, hearing unwelcome advice from our parents, or answering absent-minded, repetitive questions from a (usually) cherished spouse or partner. I always feel guilty later, even if I have pulled myself together and responded almost as graciously as Sister Benedicta. I know that, however it might appear, I have not welcomed the guest as I would welcome Jesus.

Something like this happened to me just last week. It was my turn to preside at the seven o'clock Wednesday morning service, which meant that I had hauled myself out of bed at 5:45, trekked breakfastless through the snow to an empty church, scurried around to mark the day's readings in the big Bible and prepare the altar, and then celebrated a quiet Eucharist with the usual twelve or fifteen faithful parishioners. I love this service, which is almost always a warm and cozy time with a circle of insiders. By the time I have restored order to the sacristy and hung up my vestments, Fred, one of the stalwarts who doubles as acolyte and cook, has breakfast ready downstairs in the parish hall: biscuits, scrambled eggs, plenty of coffee, and good conversation before we get on with the day.

Last Wednesday, though, one member of the congregation came back to me right after the dismissal and said, "Someone is here looking for a pastor. Do you want to see him?" I'm afraid that I answered, "No," but added immediately, "but I'll talk to him anyway." She pointed out a man waiting in the now empty, still dark church. He was youngish, neat and respectful, yet obviously troubled and overwhelmed. In other days I would have given him some money just to assuage my conscience but instead we sat down together in a pew as I listened to a rambling story of lost faith, illness, and the need to get an expensive prescription filled. I forgot my impatience and my friends already downstairs at breakfast, and just saw a wounded and fragile stranger who had wandered into my tidy space. Chuck and I prayed together, and then said good-bye. When I finished my sacristy duties and arrived downstairs, there was Chuck at breakfast, looking quite at home. "He's an operator," I decided, "or maybe just a survivor. After all, you have to be an operator just to survive on the streets." I was happy that my friends had seen nothing extraordinary in his turning up, that they had pulled up an extra chair and welcomed the stranger. He didn't look a bit like Jesus. He just looked like a young man who needed a lot of things, not all of them material.

❖ *Receiving Hospitality*
When our lives follow a predictable pattern and we live in relative comfort, it is easy to forget that we are often in need of hospitality ourselves. The first experience of this

was at the very beginning of our lives, when we were given the shelter of our mother's body. To be pregnant is to let oneself be taken over, at least for a time. The child growing in the womb gets priority over all available resources: in my childhood there was an old wives' saying, "For every child a tooth." This is no longer meaningful in our well-nourished society, but in leaner times the unborn child sapped the mother of the calcium needed for those tiny, growing bones. It is an amazing, humbling feeling to provide a sheltered space for a new person, or at least a person-in-process. I greeted each of my three immediately after birth with a mixture of surprise and recognition: "Oh, that's what you look like! I feel as if I already know you, after all this time that we've been living together. I know that you have made yourself quite at home, that you take my hospitality for granted, and that you like to take your exercise just when I am ready to sleep." This is the easiest kind of hospitality *and* the most demanding.

Jesus, who described himself as homeless, relied on the hospitality of his friends—Mary and Martha, Simon the Leper, the tax collector Zacchaeus, the Samaritan woman whom he met beside the well. He was no doubt setting us a good example as to how to behave as both host and guest: to respond easily and generously to the needs of others even as we acknowledge our own neediness and let ourselves be served. It did not take me long to learn that it is easier to be the one doing the serving, hoping to be thanked or at the very least left with a satisfying sense of my own generosity. By St. Paul's time, hospitality became inextricably linked with the perpetuation of the new church: traveling missionaries relied on a cordial reception by the local Christian community. This is clear from those passages that open and conclude his letters, those long lists of affectionate greetings to men and women, to whole households and families. Paul, who gets such bad press as a grouch and misogynist, is filled with love for his extended family in Christ.

In my own small way, I know what that must have been like. I never travel as a tourist these days, nor can I think of myself as a "business traveler." Instead, in a modest way, I am following in the footsteps of my first-century brothers and sisters. I arrive at a strange airport and stand by the baggage carousel. Neither I nor my host carries a sign, but we always find one another. Literally and spiritually, I am embraced and folded into the circle of the Christian community in that place. For a weekend or a week or maybe even two I am part of the family. We eat and pray and talk together. We share the Eucharist. Then it's off to the airport again. The greetings that continue to link us are not written on parchment but carried through space via e-mail: greet Bishop Andrew in New York . . . Sissie in Mississippi . . . Ted in the Arizona desert . . . Brother Timothy in South Africa . . . Sister Kathleen in Tennessee . . . Philip in Australia . . . Pui Fong in Hong Kong . . . Janet in England . . . Sister Johnette in Kansas. . . . The list goes on and on. I am awed by the households who have welcomed me as they would welcome Christ, loved me and cared for me, and then sent me on my way.

❖ *True Hospitality*

So what does hospitality look like in the twenty-first century? Will I know it when I see it? Is it still an obligation, or just a nice option? Not everything that calls itself hospitality would pass the test with Benedict or Paul. Ruthless business is often conducted over carefully prepared and elegantly served meals; shallow and impersonal cordiality is epitomized by the "hospitality suite" that has become a ubiquitous part of any conference or convention. There is the careful balancing of indebtedness, not just for food and drink but for favors granted and received—Is it my turn to pick up the tab or yours? God forbid that you should pay for my modest lunch two times in succession. To be sure, there are the obvious acts of hospitality, the easy, effortless ones. When I share a meal with a good friend, I am enriched by our time together, no matter who picks up the bill. The give-and-take of friendship is a win-win situation: both parties have given and received, and the line between host and guest becomes pleasantly blurred. But true hospitality is costly and does not depend on how we feel. It might mean letting go of inflated ideas of our own worth and moving to a place at the table where no one else wants to sit. Jesus reminds his friends of this: when you are invited to a party, sit in the lowest place; if that is the wrong spot for you, it will get sorted out. Your job is to be there and to be open to what might happen—perhaps you will receive and perhaps you will give.

True hospitality also means that we extend welcome to the most unlikely guests: "the poor, the crippled, the lame, and the blind" (Luke 14:13)—the very people, Jesus says, who cannot repay us. This kind of hospitality is relatively easy so long as we can assure ourselves that it is a temporary situation and that, after we have done our charitable duty, we can retreat to our own place of comfort. The identified poor are easy to spot: they live on the street, they are shabby or even disheveled, and they do not always smell very good. They are nothing like us, of course—or are they? What if this passage means extending our generous, unself-conscious hospitality to the spiritually poor, impaired, and blind among us? What if it means welcoming those among us whom everyone else is avoiding? What if it means—here Benedict is dangerously radical—meeting everyone we encounter as if they were Christ?

This is not the same as transforming ourselves into doormats. There is a fine but very firm line between willing generosity and letting ourselves be used—maybe because it brings us satisfaction to create dependency in others, maybe because we have an unhealthy desire for martyrdom and decide to hurry things along, maybe because we confuse giving ourselves with not valuing ourselves.

It is easy and tempting to sort out our priorities: this person is worthy of my attention, this person might be helpful to me as I move upward and onward, this person might at least be properly grateful, this person might be the worthy recipient of my charity while this person is quite disposable. Yet we are promised—or warned?—in Jesus' story of the incognito king that things are not what they seem and that God's standards are not the world's standards.

The unnamed author of the letter to the Hebrews knew this: "Do not neglect to show hospitality to strangers, for by doing that some have entertained angels without knowing it" (13:2). This word of advice can be comforting or alarming, depending on where we are, spiritually and geographically, at any given moment. It is hard for me to believe that I might be entertaining an angel when the volunteer for the local public television station interrupts me at the dinner hour with a phone call requesting money, or when the supermarket clerk refuses to make eye contact and leaves me feeling that I have intruded on her space. But many times we might be entertaining angels when we are too busy to notice. These hospitality angels, like the Holy Spirit, can be very subtle. Of course sometimes they are hard to miss, but all too often we just pass them by.

Dee, who answers my doctor's telephone, is one of my hospitality angels. I'm not sure that I would recognize her if I met her on the street, but just the sound of her voice makes me feel better. Then there's Veronica from Ghana. She is one of the checkers at the wildly eclectic discount grocery just up the street from the elegant gourmet shop. Her perfunctory colleagues do their job just as efficiently, but Veronica's broad smile, her collegial expressions of gratitude when I help bag the fruits and vegetables, her inquiries about my whereabouts when I am on the road—all make my encounters with her at the cash register occasions of true hospitality. I miss her on her rare days off! I remember too a very small hospitality angel. I was emerging from the jetway after a long flight when a tiny boy ran toward me with arms outstretched shouting, "Nana!" As his embarrassed mother scooped him up, she told him, "That's not Nana." I felt welcomed anyway.

When I lived in New York and rode the subway daily, I would entertain myself by speculating: Who are the angels? What am I missing? Recalling the story in Genesis where Jacob, sleeping in the desert with a stone for a pillow, looked up and saw the heavens opened and angels ascending and descending, I would occasionally look up the grimy stairs to the street and ask myself, *Which ones are the angels? Surely there must be one or two in that motley crowd.* I never knew for sure.

Questions for Prayer and Pondering

❖   What has been your experience of receiving hospitality? When have you been an honored guest, realizing that you were the guest perhaps only after the fact?

❖   Sometimes the generosity of hospitality shows itself in small things that might pass unnoticed. I remember being welcomed in the Austrian Tyrol with an enormous bunch of daisies. In German daisies are *Margareten,* just like my name. I was far from home, and when I was greeted with that huge bouquet, I laughed and cried simultaneously. What has been your experience of offering hospitality? Has it been a chore? a joy? When have you entertained angels without knowing it?

❖   Benedict tells us to greet every visitor as if that person were Christ. How can this be incorporated into your rule of life? Dig a bit, and you may be surprised by all the challenges and potentially missed opportunities.

6 ❖

Learning from
Our Enemies

❖❖❖ "What is the point," Jesus asks, "of loving only the people who love you?" This is one of his hard teachings, tucked away in the middle of the Sermon on the Mount. He makes it clear that it's not good enough to sort people into neat groups of acceptable and unacceptable, lovable and unlovable, keepers and disposables. And it's certainly not good enough to permit ourselves the luxury of hating our brothers and sisters, no matter how much we might feel that they deserve it. Love your enemies, he commands, and pray for those who persecute you.

I usually try to persuade myself that Jesus was guilty of hyperbole here, maybe overdoing it to make a point or to set a high standard. I play out little scenes in my imagination, where I discuss the situation with him in a reasonable way: "Nice idea, Jesus, and I certainly understand what you're getting at. But you cannot honestly expect me to love X, Y, or Z!" Depending on the circumstances, it might be the neighbor who permits her dog—who is the size of a small pony and has a voice like the Hound of the Baskervilles—to bark lustily at four in the morning. It might be a political leader whose views about compassion and justice are radically different from mine. It might be the serial murderer whose face is on the tabloids at the supermarket or the parent accused of unspeakable child abuse or the drunken driver who killed a little old lady on her way to the bus stop. It might be a loved one—who unthinkingly wounded me decades ago, and I remember the incident as if it were yesterday. It might be a friend who betrayed me; if we have lived long enough, we have all met Judas. Or, as I am ashamed to acknowledge even to myself, it might be a colleague or acquaintance who simply drives me crazy. So my negotiations with Jesus go something like this: "Okay, I agree that loving my enemies is a laudable goal, and I promise that I will strive to achieve it. But in the meantime, isn't ninety percent good enough? Or maybe even eighty-five?" And despite all my internal equivocation, I know that his answer is a flat no.

Yet, fallen creature that I am, I am compelled to recognize the fact of enmity. To read the Psalms on this topic is profoundly liberating, especially if we contemplate those passages we never hear in church. Remember that the Psalms are prayers offered *to* God rather than God's pronouncements on us, and as such they are powerful examples of candor, shockingly blunt communication with the God to whom all hearts are open, all desires known, and from whom no secrets are hid. They make it clear that to be human is to have enemies, to be human is to suffer from injustice and betrayal, to be human is to yearn for vengeance. The bottom line: to be human means that we are not as nice as we pretend to be. Psalm 58 is a particular favorite on those days when I feel that the world is against me. It is full of enemies who devise evil in their hearts; they are perverse, liars from birth, and venomous as serpents. The psalmist's suggestions as to how God might punish them are even better:

> O God, break their teeth in their mouths;
>   pull the fangs of the young lions, O LORD.

> Let them vanish like water that runs off;
> let them wither like trodden grass.
> Let them be like the snail that melts away,
> like a stillborn child that never sees the sun. . . .
> The righteous will be glad when they
> see the vengeance;
> they will bathe their feet in the blood of the wicked
> (Psalm 58:6–10)

The psalm ends here, and we do not have God's reaction to this satisfying diatribe!

❖ Who Are Our Enemies?

Often our enemies are faceless and far away: the people whom we have been taught to fear, the people who are very different from us, those who—we are persuaded—live only to do us harm. A common enemy can be a marvelously unifying force. So all Germans were demonized in World War I; even dachshunds fell out of favor as family pets, and Bach was suspect. I am ashamed to remember the crude but powerful propaganda prevalent during World War II that uniformly portrayed all Japanese as physically repulsive and appallingly cruel—nothing like the lovable Japanese students to whom I taught English after the war, eager to make the most of their year at an American university. For decades we feared the godless Communists, but with the collapse of the Soviet Union they ceased to be the menace of the month. So now our all-purpose enemy is grouped together under the umbrella of "terrorist." It's a big umbrella, capable of sheltering the whole Muslim world. I am not so naive as to deny that we live in a time when we appear to need enemies to understand and validate our own identity. The single-minded focus on an enemy assures us that we are righteous, that our reward will be to bathe our feet in the blood of the wicked. Ironically, we are outraged when we realize that our identified enemies have precisely the same intention toward us.

Then there are the enemies who truly wish us harm. Are we really expected to forgive them? I have never been faced with such an onerous obligation and wonder if I would be able to forgive the rapist or the murderer of my child. Yet such generous people exist, and I am humbled by their example. I am blessed to know two of them, who have managed to see a human face in the man who cold-bloodedly killed their daughter. It shames me to realize how tenaciously I cling to my resentment at the petty betrayals by a few—a very few, scattered through the decades of my life—who certainly wished me harm, but stopped far short of murder. If I took the gospel message seriously, I would see them as made in God's image, fallen but scarcely worthy of damnation. Not that such judgment would be up to me!

It is easy and convenient to assign those whom we envy to the ranks of our enemies. Envy is a murderous sin, all too often confused with jealousy. If I am jealous, my affections are skewed, and I am lacking in generosity; I want the object of my love, whatever it is, all to myself. But if I am envious, I cannot bear the other's good fortune or talent. There can be no shared enjoyment or celebration: I want to kill the object of my envy. As Ann and Barry Ulanov say in their wise book *Cinderella and Her Sisters,* "Envy wants to make something alive into something dead. Envy looks hard for evil in another person and takes great satisfaction in finding it."[6] To identify these enemies requires that we look deep within ourselves and recognize our own capacity for sin. We need to ask ourselves, What can my brother or sister possess that arouses my envy to the extent that I do not want to possess it myself, but to destroy it? And, incidentally, to destroy them in the process?

Unwittingly, we may also find ourselves identified as the enemy by those who envy us. It took me by surprise when, a long time ago, someone I worked with accused me of "wanting to destroy her." She was younger than I, rapidly climbing the professional ladder, and seemed to have it all—if I had been a little more ambitious, I would have seen her position as enviable. It had not occurred to me that I had anything she might have wanted, and I am quite sure that she did not—probably could not—believe me when I told her that I wished only well for her. The situation was smoothed over, rather like pasting wallpaper over a deep crack in the plaster, but the drop of poison remained and did its work. For the rest of the time we worked together, we were both "the enemy."

Enemies might also be those toward whom we feel contempt and cold-heartedness. Hatred is so much easier than compassion, once we let ourselves slip into it. To view the derelict, the prisoner, or the addict as the enemy permits us to distance ourselves and avoid the complex work of blending mercy with justice. It also permits us to hold on to our fear, the fear of what the "enemy" might do to us. At the same time, it permits us to ignore the very real fear that comes with recognition of our kinship, that we are all—the most saintly and the most contemptible among us—made in God's image, fallen and yet valued. I would rather not claim my kinship with the killer or the drug dealer in the maximum security prison, the deranged person begging by the subway station or even the ordinary person with extraordinarily bad luck. It is much easier and more pleasant to identify them as the enemy and then, like the priest and the Levite, pass by on the other side.

Perhaps "enemy" is too strong a term to designate the irritating people, those who get in our way, those who are simply a nuisance. We know that they cannot destroy us, nor do they want to, but they can certainly make life more difficult than it really needs to be. One of my favorite allegories of the spiritual journey is the movie *The African Queen*. That unlikely pair—a prissy Hepburn and a slovenly Bogart—undertake a perilous journey to safety in Bogart's ramshackle boat. They are shot at from riverbanks and they nearly drown navigating the rapids, but it is the flies and leeches that threaten to do them in. It is very hard to love flies and leeches, and even harder to love their human equivalents. While we need not welcome them when they threaten to drain our blood or drive us mad with bites and stings, we can at least try to see them for what they are. However annoying they might be, we need to remember that they probably intend no harm: they are behaving in the only way they can. I am almost sure that every church, office, and school has at least one or two such folk, blithely unaware of their effect on others. I confess to feeling guilty when I hide in my office or slip out the side door or procrastinate returning a phone call because I can't quite face the human equivalent of a swarm of flies or a pond of hungry leeches.

Sometimes the enemy lives very close to home, under the same roof. The book of Genesis, that great family soap opera, provides plenty of stories of intimate enmity, stories that were glossed over in my Sunday school days but provided rich material for my private reading. Just look at Abraham and Sarah, our spiritual ancestors: there was enough going on in that household to run on television for several seasons. We have no idea how Sarah felt when Abraham uprooted the family. He said it was God's command, but it must have seemed crazy to a hard-working housewife already advanced in years. And on it goes: passing Sarah off as his sister, not once but twice, so that she almost ended up in Pharaoh's harem; bitter rivalry between Sarah and Hagar; the near-sacrifice of Isaac—no mother I know would stand for that! Think of the currents of enmity rippling through that household as Jacob cheats Esau of his birthright and then goes on to cheat his father-in-law. Out of jealousy, Joseph's brothers plan to kill him and then, in a fit of compassion, decide merely to sell him into slavery.

So why should we be surprised that all too often our enemies are very near us, that domestic violence—physical and emotional—is a daily fact of life? Or that wounds and grudges lie, unacknowledged and unforgiven, just beneath the surface in our very ordinary households? "Family" is such an inviting word, typically evoking warm feelings of safety and care, but ongoing proximity is not always easy. We grate on one another; we compete with one another; we hurt and betray one another. Siblings grow up convinced that their brother or sister is the favorite child. If a marriage lasts long enough, both partners will have accumulated a store of grievances, most but not all of them petty. It is often easier to forgive the faceless enemy half a continent away than it is to look with love at the imperfect people who share our homes and who have, deliberately or inadvertently, hurt us.

Sometimes the enemy is even closer to home. It is a cliché that we are our own worst enemies; clichés and hackneyed truisms exist because they are almost always true. In his letter to the Romans, Paul speaks for all of us when he exclaims that he does not understand his own actions when he does not do what he wants to do, but rather does the very thing he hates. In our failure to love ourselves as made in God's image, we can indeed become our own worst enemies.

One of my favorite characters in the Harry Potter novels is Dobby, the servile house-elf. This small creature is so filled with self-imposed guilt, so quick with abject apologies for wrongs he has not committed, so assured of his own sinfulness that he is happy only when someone is beating him up. If no one obliges, he batters himself. I find myself wanting to reassure him, to point out to him all his good qualities: his generous nature, his indefatigable willingness to serve others, his lovable simplicity. Although he is a fictional character, something in him rings true: when we judge ourselves harshly, when we see ourselves as beyond redemption, we treat ourselves as the enemy. When we make choices that damage us, we become the enemy. Succumbing to harmful addictions, consistently failing to care for ourselves, misusing our God-given gifts, working ourselves to the point of exhaustion—all these behaviors make us our own enemy. In moments of self-awareness, we want to cry out with Paul: "Why am I doing the very thing I hate?" and then we continue to do it.

❖ *Forgiving as a Spiritual Discipline*
"What is the point," Jesus says, "of loving only the folk who are easy to love—the people who are like you, who love you in return, who will only your good, who would never do you harm? That's no challenge at all!" I try to remember this every time I pray the Lord's Prayer. Whatever words we use—"forgive us our trespasses as we forgive those who trespass against us" or "forgive us our sins as we forgive those who sin against us"—it is very easy to pray the first petition and conveniently forget the second. Of course God will forgive my sins, assuming that I am at least moderately contrite. We are praying to a loving God, after all, a God who numbers the hairs on our heads and who cares what happens to us. But what about us? Are we up to it? Can we let go of our hurts and grievances and righteous anger so that our behavior can at least be a pale reflection of the prodigally forgiving love of God?

I have never been sure what forgiveness is, and I know less and less with each passing year. But I know that it isn't cheap and it isn't easy. When it happens too soon, too painlessly, it reminds me of the too-quick healing of a wound: there is healthy new skin on the surface, but deep down the hurt is still festering. More often, the image for me is a great block of ice, melting slowly but inexorably. It cannot be hurried: there is no spiritual equivalent of the microwave. Sometimes it feels as if we are stuck, but if we let ourselves be open, the melting goes on.

We are each responsible for ourselves. Only I can forgive the sins or trespasses committed against me by another. Others can make suggestions, even voice disapproval, but I have to do the forgiving. Our relationship with our enemies is an intimate and ultimately lonely one. How we live into it is up to us. Jesus gives us a daunting example when he prays from the cross: "Father, forgive them, for they do not know what they are doing." Who are "they"? Most obviously, he is praying for his murderers—those who condemned and tortured him, and who are now killing him. He is praying for all those who hated and feared him and sought to destroy him, along with the soldiers who were "just following orders" and could not wait to divide up his clothing. What about Judas, the betrayer? He must be included—and Peter, who denied him out of fear after protesting his undying loyalty. Jesus' words from the cross deprive us of the luxury of the holdout, of hurt kept alive and our forgiveness withheld. We can no more forgive someone a little than we can be "a little bit" pregnant. Jesus did not look at the man with the hammer and say, "I forgive you, but I'm never going to forget this."

Most of our lives are lived on an embarrassingly petty scale—grudges nursed, hurts carefully tended so that they never heal. From the cross, Jesus rips our pettiness to shreds and shows us how enemies should be treated. His standard of forgiveness is radical, breathtaking, seemingly impossible. I'm not sure that I'm up to the challenge. But at least I can try.

In the meantime, it's a good idea to think about enemies from time to time, even to incorporate this reflection into my rule of life. Who might see me as the enemy? To this question, I usually answer, "Me? Who could possibly see me, hard-working and generally well-meaning *me* as an enemy?" It can be a painful exercise in self-examination to reflect on whom we might have hurt, diminished, or dismissed, intentionally or carelessly. And then to ponder: what am I going to do about it? And who are my enemies? What can I learn from them? Justly or unjustly, those who wish us harm can teach us a great deal about ourselves. Am I being condescending when I think that I am gracious? Speaking harshly and hurtfully when I think I am helpfully direct? Coldhearted when I ignore the need of a brother or sister? Arrogant when I assume that my way—as an individual or as a citizen of my country—is the best and only way? If we pay attention and are willing to look at ourselves honestly, our enemies can teach us a lot.

Questions for Prayer and Pondering

❖   Who might see you as the enemy? Can you identify people whom you have hurt or treated badly—or simply carelessly? What are you going to do about them?

❖   Who are your enemies? What can you learn from them? In what ways might your actions and words be harmful to others, even when you think you are being helpful or polite or patriotic?

❖   Are you able to pray for your enemies? Even though the psalmist gives us splendid examples of vengeful prayer and even though our righteous anger may feel very good, wishing others dead or hurt cannot really count as praying for them. How could you incorporate prayer for your enemies into your daily rule?

7

The Cultivation
of Solitude

In my younger and more judgmental days I didn't really approve of Jesus' ability to walk away from all those people who were clamoring for him, to give even his close friends the slip so that he could enjoy the luxury of solitude. Peter and his friends sometimes had to hunt him down and remind him that everyone was looking for him—there was apparently an inexhaustible supply of sick folks needing healing. But I realize now that Jesus is teaching us an important lesson: unrelenting activity cannot be sustained, at least if it is to be fruitful. There must be times of going apart, of slowing down, of being alone. Those are the liminal times, when God can be encountered in dark and desert places. In other words, these times of solitude are thin times and places: God is very close, but so is evil. Solitude can be enlivening or dangerous, threatening or reassuring, transforming and at the same time wounding. It all depends.

In our lives we experience different kinds and circumstances of solitude. Sometimes we yearn for it, when our lives are too full of activities and interaction with other people, and the pace of our days has become too fast.

Sometimes solitude is forced upon us, just as Jesus was driven into the desert after his baptism. Sometimes it comes upon us as an unwelcome surprise, when a loved one dies or we must leave the community of which we are a part. Sooner or later, most of us will taste solitude in all its guises. Surrounded by the noise and bustle of the intensive care unit, my friend Joan kept a solitary vigil while she waited for her husband to die. She resisted offers of friends to come sit with her; she was driven to live through that time by herself. "Grief," she later told me, "has its own inevitable solitude." The bleak waiting room, with its plastic chairs and old magazines, bore no resemblance to Jacob's stony desert, but it was an awesome, vulnerable place nonetheless. A year after Bill's death, Joan's solitude continues. It is not so desolate and unrelieved now, but it will be one of her dwelling places for the rest of her life.

Some of us deliberately embark on journeys of solitude, risky pilgrimages into the unknown. My colleague Lucy once drove alone across the Australian outback to Ayers Rock, the holy mountain of the Aboriginal people. All of her friends, myself included, scolded her for her imprudence. Was she crazy, traveling by herself through hundreds of miles of arid, deserted landscape? What if she had car trouble? Or ran out of gas or drinking water? Or fell among robbers? Couldn't she sign on as part of an organized tour group? That was a long time ago, and today the old road is no doubt a well-traveled highway, with amenities along the way, but at the time, Lucy's journey into solitude seemed almost mythic. It was something that she was impelled to do, not as a tourist but as a seeker. No holiday trip, it was a journey into herself, not just into the outback.

❖ *Choosing Solitude*
The cultivation of solitude may also be a spiritual discipline, part of our rule of life. We can choose to retreat, to remove ourselves from the familiar with all its demands on our time and energy, to say nothing of our mind and spirit.

Like Jesus, when the demands of others threatened to crush him, we take ourselves to "a deserted place" where perspective can be corrected and balance restored. To be sure, the very word "retreat" has overtones of the monastery and the cloister, unthinkable to some and irrelevant to others. At the other end of the spectrum, the word has been taken over by the corporate world and—too often—even by the church to designate marathon, offsite business meetings from which we return more tired than when we left home, our heads rattling with ideas, proposals, solutions, and questions. Yet a traditional retreat, which is a limited time of withdrawal to a place steeped in silence, where prayer has soaked into the very walls, can be a restorative, even life-changing experience even if it is not the path for everyone.

Last year I led a retreat for the young and youngish stay-at-home mothers of my parish. We couldn't travel far since their time away from their small children was very limited, but we managed to find a quiet space for an overnight stay at the nearby cathedral college. Some of them feared they would be herded into the chapel to talk about Christian piety for the whole time, so the best part, they told me later, was a whole afternoon with no agenda—a little patch of pure solitude. Some stayed in their rooms, where they read (maybe Scripture and maybe a best-seller they had tucked in their bag) or prayed or slept—for mothers of infants and toddlers it was absolutely the right use of this tiny taste of solitude. Another woman told me that she just sat in the cathedral and watched the changing patterns of color on its white walls, as the afternoon sun shone through the stained glass. She was a little apologetic that she had not prayed, but had "just sat there and let the space speak" to her. Another went for a walk on the busy shopping street in front of the cathedral. Despite the familiar surroundings, it was an almost exotic experience: no errands to run, nothing to buy, no stroller to push, no need to rush home to prepare dinner. She had found her bit of solitude on a noisy street, surrounded by traffic noises and by people in a hurry to get somewhere.

Of course, we can make a retreat in other ways; there are plenty of holy places without stone walls or stained-glass windows. And if we cannot manage time away, we can find our holy space without leaving home for a day or a few hours of a spring afternoon. The parenting books speak of "quality time" with our children, despite the pressure of busy schedules. Our times of solitude can be "quality time," too, even if we fit them into our limited available spaces. One of my friends, after bemoaning the laxity of her Lenten discipline, was almost rhapsodic when she told me what it was like to work in her garden in early spring, too early for blossoms and fruits. She had spent most of the time on her knees clearing out dead plants and then preparing the soil for new growth. Her back got tired, and she had dirt under her fingernails. "But it was almost like praying," she said. I commented that it was a pretty good approximation.

Then, too, there is the solitude demanded by the creative process, even if we think we could not possibly be true creators. Maybe such creativity is for a Mozart composing by candlelight in an underheated room in old Vienna or a Rilke writing his amazing elegies in a castle high above the Adriatic, but not for the rest of us. Yet even serious study is a creative process, the thoughtful reflection and hard work we need to do in order to turn knowledge into wisdom. Study can be mental if not physical solitude. I am surprised, again and again, at what a lonely work writing a book is—and how unlike other work it is. When I get around to cleaning the house or raking the leaves, it is simply a matter of getting on with it. One task follows another, and the job is done in the allotted time. But the creative process has its own rhythm of going into the desert and coming back, with its seemingly wasted empty spaces along the way that really are not wasted at all. Mentally, it demands that we go to that deserted place "somewhere else," even when the real life of family and job goes on around us. After all, Harriet Beecher Stowe wrote *Uncle Tom's Cabin* in spare moments at her kitchen table. I picture the children tugging at her skirts and the soup boiling over while she retreated to her own fruitful desert place. Without the luxury of a quiet room to herself, she was nevertheless able to find the inner solitude to create the most powerful novel of her day.

❖ The Dark Side of Solitude

Sometimes, of course, we go to great lengths to avoid solitude, and when we do surrender, we are left with no place to hide from God or from ourselves. That is why the image of the desert is so compelling: the light of day admits no shadows while the dark of night is very dark indeed. The demons of solitude came to St. Anthony in many guises— as hideous fiends, seductive women, and even as a piteous child. His biography occasionally reads like the story of a delusional hermit. My demons are not nearly so interesting, but in extended periods of living alone in our old Blue Ridge house reading, studying, and writing, I learned to expect times of existential angst and holy terror. At first this took me by surprise: there were no murderers around the house and I was safe from passing bears, who have been known to crash through flimsy doors and windows if the fruit is not stowed safely away. But then it would come upon me: an awareness of the immensity of the cosmos, the immensity of God, and my own smallness. Only in retrospect would I remember Job, whittled down to size by the divine voice from the whirlwind. I couldn't predict these nights or call them forth, but I learned to experience them with a kind of comfortable discomfort—not by turning on all the lights, but by going outdoors to sit in utter darkness.

Solitude is different from isolation. Whether we have deliberately cut ourselves off from companionship or whether we have been excluded by others, isolation deadens the soul. Solitude freely chosen can be sustaining and nourishing. Most of us need periodically to recharge our spiritual batteries. We can do this only in solitude. My cordless phone announces its need to be restored with little beeps not heard by the person on the other line; my laptop sends me a stern but friendly message on the screen that the battery is about to give out. Thus far I haven't discerned the spiritual equivalents of these warning signals that it is time to recharge, with the result that it is all too easy to keep running fast and to see refreshing solitude as self-indulgent.

The industrialized West is a busy, noisy place. The ubiquitous cell phone is emblematic: we dare never be out of touch. E-mail, a blessing for spontaneous communication, also intrudes upon our solitude. Words crowd in upon us; friends and strangers claim our attention *now*. In the olden days of writing letters with stamps on them, you could expect a week or so of grace before a reply was expected. Now I sometimes feel tethered to my electronic inbox, always delinquent, never quite caught up. Restorative time alone is hard to come by, even for the privileged and comfortable who have the luxury of a home with private rooms. What can life be like in the spiritual and physical crowding of small offices and cubicles, or even well-run and humane hospitals and nursing homes? Or for young children who, because of day care, are literally never alone?

It is too easy, however, to blame the endemic busyness of our noisy society. I know that I, at least, am complicitous. When I wrap sounds and stimuli around me like a blanket, even when I am quite alone, I know that I am resisting the vulnerable receptivity of true solitude. It might sound restful, but yielding to it is a journey into the unknown. True solitude is a state of surrender and spiritual nakedness. It requires that we let go of our fear of emptiness, our compulsion to *do* and simply allow ourselves to *be*.

❖ *Finding a Healthy Balance*
As in other areas of physical, emotional, and spiritual self-care, a rule helps us to find and maintain a healthy balance. There are times when I want to be alone simply because I am tired. There are times when I want to be alone because I find those I am with annoying or overly demanding. Well and good—such times of solitude can be restorative or at least can avert emotional fireworks in the family or the workplace. But the place of solitude in a rule of life goes deeper: it is our deliberate removal of ourselves from the workaday scene so that we can be open and spiritually uncluttered—at least for a little while. We can be totally present to ourselves even as we put ourselves out of the way. We can give our undivided attention to whatever God might send us—be it fascinating temptations, sustaining and comforting insights, or simple silence.

It helps to have a *place* where you can be alone because solitude is spatial as well temporal. In his Rule Augustine states:

> In the oratory, no one should do anything that conflicts with the use of the building, which is implied by its name, so that if those who happen to be free wish to pray there outside the fixed hours they would not be hindered by anyone who might think of doing something else there. (chp. II)

This was apparently a first: there is no previous monastic record of setting aside a special room or building for solitary prayer. Most of us are not privileged to have our own private oratory, and even our churches are frequently busy, bustling places with no quiet corner set aside solely for prayer. Yet we can create our own places—sometimes desert places—where we seek solitude.

Sometimes these are special places quite separate from our homes and churches, such as an isolated cabin or a garden in the woods. Oratories do not have to be in designated sacred spaces. I live a subway ride away from the

National Gallery of Art. My visits there fall into two distinct categories. When I am with others, I feel and behave like a tourist. It is an enjoyable experience, sometimes intellectually stimulating, but never profound. When I am by myself, however, I know that I am in a sacred place. I seek out my old friends—often a Saint Anne altarpiece or the Raphael Madonna—and just sit with them in solitude, even though schoolchildren are swarming through in groups along with tourists from all over the world, and the guard by the door is looking apprehensive at someone who is staying too long looking intently at one thing—*not* normal museum behavior. Literal solitude is not required; I am in a sacred space in the midst of a crowd.

Nor is beauty essential, though it can be helpful. When I lived in New York City, my daily subway ride was sometimes, though to be sure not always, a restorative desert time. Anyone who knows the New York subway, either from experience or the movies, knows that it in no way resembles a traditional holy space. But it can be a desert. Instead of fierce wild beasts, the rider is surrounded by all sorts and conditions of people, some of alarming or at least unusual appearance. Instead of silence, there is the screeching roar that is like none other, along with unintelligible loud announcements from time to time. It is an ideal desert, so long as you pray with your eyes wide open and your wits about you.

These days my desert spaces, aside from Jenkins Hollow in the Blue Ridge and the National Gallery, are likely to be an airport or a plane. These places are strangely timeless, despite schedules, delays, and canceled flights. I am powerless: there is nothing to be done beyond showing up, possibly waiting in a large drab space, and then being herded into a small drab space. There may be hundreds of people around me, but I am essentially alone. The time spent there can be tedious—or it can be holy. It all depends.

We can find solitude in our cars and in our backyards, when we run or swim or walk. We can find it when we wake in the night, in our waiting and in our watching. We need only pay attention, let ourselves be vulnerable, and enter in. Solitude is like the gradual clearing of the churned-up waters of a pond—a lovely, clean, woodland pond, not one in a city park with old sneakers and potato chip wrappers floating in it. Whatever floats in the water is good, organic, the stuff of life. But for the water to be clear the organic matter must be allowed to sink to the dark bottom of the pond. Not a bad place, but a hidden one.

✣

Questions for Prayer and Pondering

❖　Time alone can be nourishing or depleting. What constitutes a retreat for you? Where are your desert places?

❖　Our personal temperament plays a role in our need for solitude. For some of us—the serious introverts—solitude is life-sustaining. For extroverts, on the other hand, it can seem unnecessary or even frightening. Do you welcome or fear solitude? Do you build regular times of solitude into your day? Why and when?

❖　Time and space to be alone can be a great luxury. Perhaps you thirst for solitude and it eludes you. For the mother of young children, the student in a college dorm, or the nursing home resident, solitude seems impossible. If you feel similarly hemmed in, what can you do about it? What are your inner resources?

8

Living in Awareness

It's hard to find anyone who is against prayer so long as it is done in good taste and doesn't interfere with real life. In times of earthquake, flood, and fire our political leaders solemnly assure us of their "thoughts and prayers"—it brings out the cynic in me, but who knows? And who knows what they mean by prayer? There are plenty of times when I would be hard put to explain my own imperfect practice of prayer to someone who did not believe in it. Yet these pronouncements seem so cheap, so undemanding, offered in the same way we invite the most casual acquaintance to "have a nice day." True prayer cannot be offhand, something to be done and then set aside. It is a commitment to be taken with the utmost seriousness, the very foundation of any rule of life. In Benedict's Rule prayer is the Work of God—*opus Dei*. Life in the monastery was centered and built upon the round-the-clock, ongoing repetition of the Psalms, and the brothers were able to get through all of the Psalms in the course of a week and then begin the cycle again. I suspect that some of them were sleepy, and some were bored, and some could not control their wandering thoughts. Their days were filled with manual labor and study, but prayer was their real work, and their days were soaked in it. They were living in awareness.

It has taken me most of a lifetime to grasp that saturation in the Psalms or in any other "method" of prayer is not really what it is about. A life of prayer is much more than a devotional life confined to specific practices at specific times, however helpful, indeed necessary they might be. I am missing the point if I limit my understanding of prayer to some sort of spiritual regimen, that is, if I let myself get caught up in the specifics of the "how" and the "when" to the neglect of the all-embracing "why" and "who." Then my prayer risks becoming mechanical and routine, a task—not the ongoing work of a lifetime—to be done and then ticked off the list.

The shelf beside my rocking chair is crowded with a motley collection of books on ways of praying. In its variety it rivals the collection of dog-eared cookbooks downstairs in the kitchen. Both mini-libraries have been useful to me, undergirding as they do two important areas of my life, but I know that I could and would go on praying and cooking quite satisfactorily without them. They are peripheral, not essential, to the real work. After years in the kitchen, I still like to read cookbooks and maybe even pick up a few ideas here and there. Why not a dash of cardamom or coriander in the *arroz con pollo* instead of the customary cumin? Maybe I can cut some calories by using yogurt instead of sour cream. And the aging culinary radicals of the Moosewood Collective can make even beets interesting!

My use of the old books baffles my husband, however. By the time I have finished my subjective and highly selective reading of a recipe, practically none of the original ingredients remains. Measurements are imprecise, bordering on the slapdash. Why, he wonders, do I need the tattered book propped on the counter while I dart around the kitchen? I try to explain that cooking, at least my kind of cooking, is more than following a recipe. It's a state of mind. The real work of chopping and stirring and blending is a liberating experience, bearing not the slightest resemblance to my laborious following of Julia Child, decades ago, when *Mastering the Art of French Cooking* was Holy Writ for the young housewife.

By contrast, I have come in retrospect to admire the imprecision of my mother's ways in the kitchen. When I begged her for the secret of the very rich biscuits that held up the strawberries in the shortcake, she would simply tell me, "You just make the dough very short," meaning that you worked into it huge amounts of butter and probably never the same amount two times in succession. There is a certain amount of necessary lore undergirding the art—or sacrament—of food preparation. The lore is useful, like the basic rules of English grammar, but it can take us just so far. Another ingredient is vital for the parsing of sentences or the creation of the perfect shortcake. Not to be confined to the pages of a book, this ingredient has much more to do with attentiveness, loving awareness, and letting go.

When prayer is an integral part of our lives, then we have embarked on a vastly enriched way of life. We live in conversation with God, probably talking a little less than before and also remembering to listen. Some of us have known this intimacy all our lives, praying before we have a name for it. I confess a bit of envy for some of my youngest friends, the three- and four-year-olds I meet in the children's service at our church. Unlike me at their age, their hearts are wide open, and they are on first-name terms with God. Others of us, like my old friend Gwen, have been overtaken later in life by a sudden awareness of God. Gwen was not struck blind and knocked to the ground, like Saul in his transformation to Paul. Instead, she was sitting placidly on the porch of her modest house when she was flooded with an awareness of what Meister Eckhart calls God's *is-ness*. Outwardly she looks the same—a slightly forbidding retired high school teacher— but her life was changed on that quite ordinary summer afternoon. I have always thought that her experience was more interesting than mine. Instead of bowling me over, God just crept up on me: somehow, I'm not sure when or how, my way of praying moved from conscientiously saying the right words at the right time to living in awareness.

Prayer is also a work of love, demanding our commitment and refusing to be confined to specific times and places while "real life" waits for us at the chapel door. Living in awareness is a full-time commitment: we must be on the lookout for the Holy Spirit in the most unlikely places, be conscious of the wonder of creation when we contemplate the night sky, or admire the chutzpah of a tough but tenacious weed that pushes its way through a crack in the pavement. Living in awareness means that spiritually speaking we are on high alert.

This understanding came to me gradually after one of my visits to a monastic community. The pace of common prayer now is more humane that in Benedict's day: so far as I know, no brother or sister feels compelled to stagger out of bed in the watches of the night to head for the chapel. But the repetition of the Psalms remains at the heart of their piety, and I found myself put off by the veritable flood of words, said or chanted in a monotone. Psalms just rolled on and on and on. My heart would sink when I would turn the page of the breviary and see yet another acre of verse to be got through before the office ended.

Eventually, however, I learned that I didn't have to wrestle with deep theological meaning or call up some mystical fervor within myself. It was enough to let the psalms sink into me, or perhaps I sank into them. Now and then a word or phrase might capture my imagination, and my thoughts could wander for a bit; more frequently scraps of Scripture would embed themselves in my thoughts and follow me around all day. It took me a while to decide that this counted as praying, but now I find it comforting in the truest sense of the word and oddly entertaining. It is as if I have been invited into an informal conversation with God or maybe with myself—all quite easy, no concern about making points or proving anything, just a gentle way of being rather than doing. So long as I resist all the distracting inner noises, the conversation is ongoing, with comfortable patches of silence accompanied by bursts of awareness that are sometimes reassuring and sometimes startling. There are times when I tell myself, *But you knew that all along! Why didn't you know that you knew it?*

❖ *Prayer as the Work of God*
The very term "work of God" suggests so many things: I think of obligation, responsibility, and repetitiveness. A task can be accomplished quickly, and then it is done, but work is ongoing. Ideally we should love our work, or at the very least be convinced that it is worth doing. Work is not always interesting or immediately rewarding; sometimes it is downright drudgery. We tire, we wonder why and how we have committed ourselves, we may even despair, but we keep on working. Sometimes we work alone, and sometimes our work is shared with others. In the course of a lifetime, we may experience many kinds of work: manual labor and menial chores, work that challenges our minds and work that deadens them, work that is important to our own well-being and the well-being of others and work that seems embarrassingly trivial, but (we persuade ourselves) is nevertheless somehow worthy and must be accomplished.

For many of us it is alarming to think about our daily prayer as work. Do we really need to take on more of it? Surely prayer requires an altered state of consciousness or some special spiritual gifts that have eluded us ordinary folk. Prayer, if we go beyond those glib assurances that we are keeping someone "in our thoughts and prayers," is a tough subject. Too often we assume that it is the province of the specialist, the spiritually gifted, the officially recognized saint or the guru—the picture of Bernini's statue of St. Teresa in ecstasy comes to mind. How on earth can praying in the kitchen or on the bus or maybe lying awake at night come up to *that?* I remember offering a Lenten course once where I wanted to stress the ordinariness and everydayness of our prayer. One of the younger participants, who in his not-too-distant college days had experimented with a chemical approach to the numinous, was disappointed that I could not guarantee a mind-boggling mystical experience by the third session. What we were offering on those Wednesday evenings in the church basement probably seemed so very ordinary and too much like work.

Years ago Dr. Benjamin Spock's *Baby and Child Care* was *the* parenting bible, not quite handed down by God on stone tablets, but coming very, very close to divinely ordained pronouncements. It was a good book, and a comforting one. Right at the beginning, he offered strong words of reassurance to anxious new mothers and fathers: you know more than you think you do, even if you have never been left alone with a screaming seven-pound stranger before. I realize now that this was a profound spiritual truth, applicable to all sorts of life's challenges but especially to our life of prayer. As yearners and seekers, we all know more than we think we do. In our own way, we can figure out how to go about the work of God. In other words, we can figure out how to feel safe and free as we grow in comfort with the practice of prayer.

"Practice" is an important word here. It suggests that prayer is something that we do over and over, for the rest of our lives. Some words from Artur Rubenstein's autobiography came to me the other day when I was musing about this mysterious work. At the time of his writing he was the foremost pianist in the world and could fill a recital hall just by showing up. So I was surprised and a tad disappointed when he confessed that he disliked practice and that he sometimes cheated by excessive use of the pedal. If you are not a pianist, you should know that holding down the pedal through a passage of notes creates a quite pleasant blur of sounds. The expert is not fooled, but we ordinary folk don't know the difference.

It has taken me a while to realize that Rubenstein could as well have been talking about any kind of meaningful work, including the work of God. At first I wanted to excuse him: he was a renowned musician—why on earth did he need to keep practicing? Surely he was entitled to slack off a bit and coast on his reputation. Maybe he was getting bored with Chopin and could find nothing new in his music. Yet even as he cheated—primarily himself—he recognized the need for the musician's equivalent of a rule of life. His fingers might fly over the keyboard because of his innate giftedness; but that innate giftedness could come to fruition only because of his lifelong commitment to the hard work of practice. Like the rest of us, he could coast for a while, but he knew that too much lazy use of that pleasantly blurring pedal had placed him on a slippery slope.

Even those of us who are not Rubensteins know that faithful practice is rarely an ecstatic experience. There are, of course, those times of breakthrough, when we are aware that we have reached a new place or that stubborn old obstacles have just melted away. But most of the time we just keep at it and, unlike my disappointed young man in the church basement, we know that it is quite unlikely that we will be magically transported to another realm.

Similarly, our practice of prayer must be independent of our emotional state. Naturally we want prayer to be exhilarating: I want it to make me feel good and to leave me with the assurance that I have logged on to God's website and gotten through immediately. Yet all of us experience those dry times when we don't feel like praying, when there are too many other things demanding our attention, when God seems distant, when we are not sure that we believe in God, or even that God exists. Having a regular time and place for prayer can be a great help here: we turn up regularly whether we feel like it or not. In other words, we keep our appointment with God with the same degree of conscientiousness that we bring to our appointments with our boss or our psychotherapist or our spiritual director or the plumber who comes to unclog the sink.

This does not pose a great problem in our common prayer so long as we manage at least to show up at the appointed times of worship. We can be physically present at a liturgy while our minds are a thousand miles away, busy making a grocery list or planning a trip, being appalled by the sermon or wondering why on earth *that* hymn was chosen. Our solitary prayer is different. It may feel like a rote exercise, something to be endured so we can get on with the rest of the day. We may yearn for a mountaintop experience and find ourselves day after day stuck at the foot of a very small hill. It took me a long time to realize that practically no one *lives* on top of the mountain; even visitors there are a rare sight and don't linger long.

❖ *Practicing Prayer Daily*
It helps to have a set time and place for our prayers. I doubt that any of us has a private oratory, nor are any bells ringing in our houses, but it is helpful to have a time and place for praying. Mine is a corner of my study, where I can sit in my grandmother's rocking chair with a favorite icon on the bookshelf at my elbow. I sit there to read, too, and to listen to music, but essentially it is my prayer corner. It's important, too, to recognize what is our best time of day. Much as I like the idea of closing a busy day with a kind of prayerful retrospective, all too often I find myself much too sleepy to do more than commend myself to God for the night. Morning is another matter—first a cup of coffee and a perusal of the *Post*. This might seem like putting current events ahead of God, but I find it helpful to have some sense of what is going on in the world before I settle into my rocker. The point, of course, is this: when are you most capable of paying attention? When are distrac-

tions and interruptions least likely to creep into the silence? When I worked at the seminary I liked to arrive very early for some reflective time in my office. So I came to be good friends with Mr. Blue, the night watchman, who was still on guard, reading his Bible at the front desk when I arrived. On one challenging winter day, when the sidewalks were ice-coated and the wind was piercing, I skated through the door and greeted Mr. Blue with "Oh ye ice and snow." Without skipping a beat he joined in, "Praise ye the Lord." We were joking about one of the more difficult aspects of God's creation. But it was a prayer all the same, a good-natured tongue-in-cheek prayer of thanksgiving for the things we would prefer to do without.

If we live in awareness, prayer will also punctuate our day, weave through it, and sanctify the most ordinary times and places. Pray in the shower, and remember your baptism; give thanks for the abundance of clean water, and remember the suffering of those stricken by drought. Pray in the kitchen, and spin off some intercessions and thanksgivings while you wait for the big pot of water to boil so that you can drop the pasta in. Pray when you are stuck in traffic, or interminably on hold while being reassured at regular intervals that your call is important. Pray when you hear the siren of a rescue vehicle. If you are brave, send up a prayer when you are approached by a street person. It won't make your life easier, because you will be forced to see a person created in God's image, but it can do your soul a world of good.

While we may be more inclined to remember to send up a little prayer when a funeral procession passes or an ambulance goes howling by, we can also be prayerfully aware of the bits of joy that surround us—big white bows on the church door mean that two people are committing their lives to each other in the sight of God, winsome babies riding in supermarket baskets remind us of the ongoing newness of creation. The amazing upward drift of the cherry blossoms outside my window each spring, caught in a sudden gentle gust of wind, is like a glimpse of God. When we live in awareness, bits of gratitude will mark our day. When we let ourselves pay attention, we are overwhelmed by the abundance that surrounds us: clean water flowing from the tap; food that not only nourishes us but tastes good; a warm, clean bed; friends who love us; work that sustains us; beauty that surrounds us.

When we live in a state of heightened perception, we will also find ourselves breathing prayers of intercession throughout the most ordinary day, beginning with that first cursory look at the morning newspaper. I am learning to pay attention to those random flashes that pop into my mind. When I think of someone, right down the street or halfway round the world, I know that a prayer is needed. So, in addition to a prayer, I try to send a note or an e-mail or a phone call. This may be serendipity or just plain chance, but I am convinced that it is the action of the Holy Spirit weaving us together in that strong web that holds us up and reminds us that we cannot manage on our own.

In the course of a day we can get through the five "standard forms" of prayer without even trying. Adoration, which is my response to the cloud of cherry blossoms; thanksgiving for things great and small, from the joy of a hot shower to the restoration of health and energy after last winter's illness; confession when I caught myself in barely suppressed impatience at an incompetent store clerk obviously trying her hardest; intercessions popping up all over the place; and, of course, petitions—my own prayers for all my needs. But there is one more form of prayer that is easily overlooked: the prayer of self-offering. Martin Luther reputedly began each day by signing himself with the cross. Wordlessly, he was reminding himself that he was not his own person, but rather that he belonged to God. Brother Martin was on to something. When we consciously give ourselves to God before plunging into the complexities of the day, when we specifically offer our thoughts, our words, our actions, and our worries, we have laid a foundation of awareness for the coming day.

There are many paths to living in awareness but no simple recipe: temperament and circumstances mean that what is right for me now may not be the fruitful path for my neighbor. The good folk who have it all figured out make me very anxious; we can get so caught in the "how" of prayer that we forget that it is simpler than that: prayer is a state of attentiveness, of openness, of letting go of all our distractions. So the prayer of constant awareness is a prayer of boldness and surrender. The work of God is deceptively easy; it is also incredibly difficult.

Questions for Prayer and Pondering

❖ What do you mean by prayer? How do you image God? To whom are you praying? What is your way of praying, your rhythm? Do you pray for yourself?

❖ Do you have a regular time and place for prayer? Do you look forward to that time, or is it just another chore? Do you miss it when you are not able to keep that time on a particular day?

❖ Are you burned out in your prayer—or perhaps poised on a threshold of some kind? Should you hang in with your present disciplines or look for new ways? Are you stuck in ways that you learned years ago in Sunday school or your confirmation class? What about thinking of prayer as a challenge and an adventure?

❖ Are you in the habit of giving thanks? When do prayers of thanksgiving well up for you? For what do you give thanks most often?

9 ❖

Hard Times

One of my favorite prayers, attributed to St. Augustine, is an all-embracing night prayer that is one way of turning the cares of the day over to Christ before we go off-duty. So we pray especially for those "who work, or watch, or weep this night"; we pray for the sick, the weary, the dying, the suffering, and the afflicted. That would seem to cover just about everyone who might need our prayers, but then comes the final, surprising petition: "shield the joyous." What are we praying for? If nothing else, these three little words remind us of the inevitability of hard times. They remind us of the innocence, the sheer giftedness, the not-knowing of joy. It may be fleeting or long-lived, but pure joy is fragile, to be held carefully and to be cherished. It would be cruel to burst the iridescent bubble, cruel even to remind the joyous that hard times lie ahead. It is enough merely to ask God to shield them.

The words of that prayer popped into my mind when I officiated at my son's wedding. Maybe it was because the bride and groom were closer to me than the usual wedding couple, maybe because—like any mother—I wanted them to live happily ever after, maybe because they were so radiantly in love. At any rate, that prayer to "shield the joyous" sprang unbidden into my mind when they held hands and vowed fidelity to each other "for better for worse, for richer for poorer, in sickness and in health" until they are parted by death. Those are heavy vows, but it was hard to imagine that the sun would ever cease to shine on these two young people whose joy seemed so strong that it was in no need of shielding.

These words came back to me six years later, however, when their newborn son suffered a series of frightening episodes in his first week: he would simply stop breathing. For what seemed like an eternity, but was actually only a few months, they struggled to absorb the medical reports and wondered whether this brand-new life might be shortened or impaired by some neurological accident. All their fears proved groundless, but something changed in both of them during that hard time, and I understood why the joyous need to be shielded. They are still joyous people, but now there is a dark thread woven into the tapestry of their joy. We do not talk about it, but I suspect that they have grown in compassion and, most certainly, in an awareness of the fragility of life. Sometimes, perhaps always, faith cannot mature without a passage through dark times.

The other prayer that always comes to me when I reflect on the hard times that erupt, unwelcome and undeserved, into our lives is a petition in the Lord's Prayer. Traditionally we pray "Lead us not into temptation" but I much prefer the contemporary version, "Save us from the time of trial." In other words: please don't give us more than we can handle. "Temptation" sounds a little racy; "trial" is far weightier and grim. No fun or titillation there—times of trial just have to be lived through. "Please, God," we pray, "don't send us more than we can manage. We'll do just fine with the joy, but shield us from those times and places when nothing seems to be working, when our prayer is sterile and life is bleak." Some of life's hard times are predictable, even as they are unavoidable. Debilitating illness, bereavement, heartbreak, loss of mean-

ingful work, isolation, poverty, unremitting physical or
emotional pain—all of us will taste suffering in some form.
Sooner or later, times of trial will come upon us.
I am awed and helpless when confronted by another's
inexplicable, devastating suffering. Cheap and easy words
of reassurance are obscene in the face of crushing desolation, so I struggle to understand what is expected of me
and how I might bring comfort or at least not add my bit
of mindless cruelty. Despite all our attempts at reconciling
the goodness of God with the evil we encounter, suffering
remains a mystery. The culpability of our first parents, particularly of poor, put-upon Eve who got blamed for the
Fall, no longer convinces me—if it ever did. Nor does the
idea of a punitive God dealing out punishment to disobe-
dient children. I remember reading heavy theological
books that claimed to make sense of Pol Pot and genocide
in Rwanda, serial killers and abused children, incurable
cancer and the immunodeficiency virus. I even wrote a lot
of unmemorable little term papers, trying to do in a few
pages what Milton attempted in *Paradise Lost:* to justify the
ways of God to man. In my more pious moments, especially when life is good and the sun is shining, I can buy
the party line. But then there come times when there is no
reassuring explanation, only a great, echoing "Why?"
Suffering is often only a mystery too deep to be plumbed.

These times are a challenge to our faith and to the very
notion of a rule of life, especially if we view our rule as a
kind of spiritual MapQuest downloaded from some celes-
tial source, with precise directions for the turning of each
corner, estimated times en route, and the assurance of
arrival at our destination on time. Instead, we find ourselves on a poorly marked or disappearing path with misleading signs, or none at all.

This realization came to me powerfully when I met
with Janice, a woman who was dying by inches from Lou
Gehrig's disease. She could still breathe and eat, but she
knew that inevitably those vital systems would shut down

and she would die. In the meantime, as her treacherous body betrayed her in great ways and small, I knew that she had gone to a place that I could visit only in imagination. How could I assure her that she was not really lost to God, and that the systems of her faith were infinitely stronger than the systems of her failing body? What could I possibly say to her that would not be shallow and false? She had come to me as the local "God-person," I suspect, because her own prayer had dried up.

We talked for a while, and then I sat beside her wheelchair, held her hands, and waited for the right words to come. They never did. I could only wait with her in silence. Our meeting was almost a year ago. I'm not sure whether I shall hear from Janice again, since she came to me seemingly from nowhere and then disappeared again. I think that she turned to the church because she had run out of other options and decided that a little holy conversation could do no harm. I may have failed some test, particularly if she had hoped for a wonder worker. I am sure that she will haunt my prayers, which can do no harm and might even contribute to her healing, although not to her cure.

❖ *The Dry Seasons*
These "hard times" of desolation and aridity in our prayer are easy to understand when they are connected with identifiable times of suffering in our lives. More confusing and in some ways more difficult are those times when, for no apparent reason, our prayer turns dry and meaningless.

In the ordinary course of our days, prayer usually brings us comfort; we feel that our thoughts and words are directed to the God who made and knows us, the God who wills only good for us. At least some, if not most, of the time, we can believe that we are seen and heard. Sometimes there is a powerful sense of God's loving presence. More often the experience is less dramatic but equally reassuring: whatever form or pattern our prayer might take, it anchors us. Our days are built around it; our interactions with our neighbors are colored by it; the ordinary is sanctified by it.

Inevitably, though, even if we are persistent and faithful, there will come a time when God seems not to be listening or speaking to us. We have entered a desert time. Maybe our icons—our windows to God—have turned into idols. That is, the form of our prayer has become more important than the prayer itself, or at the very least no longer serves. We can find ourselves attributing almost magical power to our methods of centering prayer, Ignatian meditation, or reading the daily offices of Morning and Evening Prayer, thereby ignoring God's invitation to risk openness and follow new paths. We can become so preoccupied with following our rule of life that we can forget where we are going.

And then the inner scolding voice takes over: "This wouldn't be happening if I were doing it right. Something is wrong. My prayer has become dull and dry; it doesn't even seem like prayer. It has become a mechanical, meaningless rote exercise." Bottom line: we find ourselves in a desert place, and we're not quite sure how we got there. Unlike the holy people of the fourth and fifth centuries, we have not sought this desert, and we most assuredly do not want to be there. The time of darkness and dryness may come gradually or suddenly as a surprise, and most certainly as a disappointment. It is easy to blame ourselves and fail to see this desert time as an unavoidable stage, not really as empty as it might seem, but rather an important part of the journey.

We may feel bored: we keep going through the motions, yet nothing is happening. Even flossing our teeth or running on our treadmill makes more sense. At least those dull bits of routine can be counted upon to contribute to our physical well-being. Our words of prayer may seem dry and empty. When we seek inner silence, our thoughts run in increasingly meaningless circles. We may feel angry, betrayed by God or someone—a figment of our imagination?—who has led us down the garden path and then disappeared. At the very least, we feel like victims of a cruel joke.

It is hard to grasp not only the inevitability but also the necessity of those times when our prayer no longer "works." It is hard to believe that times of apparent emptiness can be a necessary condition for growth. Spiritually, as in all sorts of other ways, too often we try to live by the go-getter motto, "Every day in every way I get better and better." All we need to do is to keep marching upward and onward. In the dry times God has got our attention. What if self-improvement isn't really the reason we should even bother to pray? Or what if our attempts to use prayer as a kind of magic to appease an angry deity and fend off destruction are misguided? We might be going through the motions of praying, but are actually staying on the surface and avoiding the depths in order to avoid all the questions and the dark places, the uncertainties and the open doors.

❖ *Hanging In and Hanging On*
The writers in the Christian tradition would say that those of us nourished and sustained by our ongoing life of prayer during hard times, whether we are young or old and however we came to it, are experiencing "consolation." On first hearing the word in this context, it struck me as strange and a little trivial, like sympathy cards with lilies and pious sayings for the bereaved. Yet the more I reflect on the term, it seems very apt. "Consolation" has an aura of safety, of being held and strengthened. When we are consoled, we know that we are not alone, and that makes all the difference.

When the time of trial comes upon us, we feel desperate and alone. We want to cry, "O God, you are my God; eagerly I seek you; my soul thirsts for you, my flesh faints for you, as in a barren and dry land where there is no water" (Psalm 63:1). The psalmist is crying out from the depths of the time of trial, a desolate cry for help before sinking in apathy. I can scarcely read these few lines of this psalm without wandering off to the kitchen for a drink of water or a cup of tea. Maybe I am distracted or procrastinating, but much more likely my body is reacting to the image of slowly drying up in an endless desert.

So what do we do in the dry and barren times, when our prayer feels pointless and futile? First of all, we recognize what is happening. This sounds easy, but is too often the most difficult step to take. Perhaps the time of trial "just happens," or perhaps something is shifting in us and we need a fallow time to prepare for growing to new depths. The further we move from our agricultural roots, the harder it is to understand and appreciate the necessity of times of fallowness, that plants actually *need* night and winter if they are to flourish, that living creatures—plant and animal—gestate in darkness. Then we need to be persistent, even when prayer seems insipid and pointless. The psalmist can be a great teacher here who knows all about hard times and does not hesitate to complain of God's inattention: "Answer me, when I call, O God.... Why do you stand so far off, O LORD, and hide yourself in time of trouble?" (Psalm 4:1, 10:1).

Part of our own rule of life might be to write our own psalms in those times when God is far away, to let go of our grown-up inhibitions and complain out loud about our sense of injury and unfairness, our mistreatment. Children secure in their parents' love are expert at this. I can recall the times when my own three made quite clear to me their sense of injustice: "You don't trust me.... You never listen to me.... You treat me like a baby.... You never let me do anything.... You never really loved me.... I didn't ask to be born." This familiar chorus of lament that almost every parent has heard is worth trying with God as well, whose patience and wisdom are infinite.

The good news of the Psalms is that they are real, they recognize the desolation of the depths, and in the end God usually comes through. We have only the *appearance* of abandonment, which does not necessarily make it easy or pleasant. But the message is clear: hang in and hang on. It is surely no accident that monastic spirituality is rooted in the ongoing repetition of the Psalms, over and over and over again, through tedium and exaltation, through good times and hard times. Eventually the words burn themselves onto our spiritual hard drives, doing their sustaining work even when nobody notices.

Most of all it is the company of each other that helps us get through those hard times. We can take turns carrying one another—I can pray for Janice when she has given up on praying for herself. On the other hand, my friend Anona has rescued me more times than she realizes when my own life turns into a dry and barren land where there is no water. So we form a great chain, linked together like mountain climbers. Or maybe we are all holding hands in a great circle dance. None of us is important, and all of us are. It takes us all to keep the dance going. Even if we are tone-deaf or have two left feet, the dance goes on.

Questions for Prayer and Pondering

❖   Take a moment to read Psalm 102. This psalm is the prayer of someone who is experiencing a time of desolation and despair, but it ends on a note of strength and confidence: the psalmist's suffering is not denied or minimized, but perspective is restored. What words in this psalm resonate with your own experience of suffering?

❖   Reflect on those hard times that you have experienced or are perhaps experiencing now. Can you see anything good that might come from it? (Be honest! This is no place for greeting-card sentimentality.) Now write your own psalm in your own language. Don't make it nice— make it real. Then keep it with you for handy reference.

❖   Those experts who would help us prepare for disaster offer lists of supplies to have on hand before calamity strikes: bottles of water, flashlights, extra batteries, and duct tape. As you prepare your rule, what might be the spiritual equivalents of these supplies needed for disaster? Where might you be guided and strengthened by your past experiences?

On Common Ground

❖❖ September 11 was a bright, clear day in Washington, D.C. It was also a Tuesday, so except for a very sparsely attended service of Morning Prayer, no liturgies were scheduled at our church until the evening Eucharist. The officiant was probably alone in the chapel reading the appointed psalm for the day when the first tower was struck. Yet by noon it was clear that we all needed the comfort of each other, so everyone in the building huddled together near the front of the church to celebrate the Eucharist. I remember sitting beside our musician, John, who claims not to have a pious bone in his body and who says he never comes to church except when he has to come to work. This was not a time to be alone, so we sat with shoulders touching, unashamedly wiping away tears now and then. We haven't talked about it much in the years since, but for me at least our friendship changed and deepened that day. We had leaned on each other and dispelled a little bit of the terror that filled the air. That evening the church was filled. I recognized many of the people as our regular congregation, but there were others who must have seen the lights on and the doors open, and who simply walked in. We sang safe old familiar hymns, said the prayers that needed to be said, and then shared the bread and the wine.

My experience was replicated in churches all over the country on that day and in the days and weeks that followed. Even cynics were yearning for some ritual to mark a time of fear and grief, and nonbelievers were drawn to the comfort of a sacred space. Optimists saw the beginning of another Great Awakening, but realists were not surprised that fervor diminished and attendance declined once some sort of normalcy resumed in the daily routine across the country.

The experience of those first frightening days after the attack was a reminder of how deeply we yearn for sacred spaces, those mysterious thin places where earth and heaven seem almost to meet. I encountered my first holy space a long time ago in a visit to Cholula, not far from the much larger city of Puebla in Mexico. It was a hot sunny Sunday; the streets were filled with families enjoying their day off. Despite our serviceable Spanish, my husband and I were obviously foreign sightseers. A serious little boy, nine or ten years old, perhaps the chief support of his family, attached himself to us as guide as we explored the ancient city.

Even in the bright spring sunshine, surrounded by people selling sodas and tiny packages of Chiclets (a favorite offering of Mexican street vendors in those days), I felt chilly and even a little bit awed that somehow this site had for millennia drawn seekers after the numinous. From the guidebook I knew that what initially appeared to be a hill was really a pyramid, a huge temple complex built over centuries by the Aztecs and the people who had preceded them. When Cortés arrived in 1519, he massacred the inhabitants of the city and vowed to build a Christian church on the site of each Aztec temple. He managed to erect fewer than fifty, but Cholula remains a city of churches and hidden holy places. I shall probably never return, but something tells me that even with a Starbucks in the plaza and a Wal-Mart on the outskirts, it will still feel like a sacred space.

Much closer to home is the great cathedral in the city where I now live. It is within walking distance of my house, so it is a pleasant diversion to stroll through the gardens and then sit for a while in the great Gothic structure, still too white and new to look quite authentic but nevertheless a place of extraordinary beauty. It sits high on a hill—perhaps a thin place chosen by someone of mystical bent, or perhaps the founders simply wanted their great church to tower over this determinedly secular city built on a swamp. When I first claimed this city as my own, I was irritated by the tourists, but over the years I have come to see them with different eyes: whatever their faith or lack of faith, they have sought out a sacred space. To be sure, often it is part of a packaged tour, but as they listen intently to the purple-garbed docent leading them around, they are visibly awed by their surroundings.

No congregation was present when YHWH spoke to Moses from the burning bush and commanded him to remove his sandals, for he was standing on holy ground. No doubt either pious tradition or the tourist industry has located the precise site of this meeting, but Scripture does not tell us of any structure created to mark the site and the bush has long ceased to burn. It is more reassuring when our sacred spaces are clearly marked and easily accessible. Even those who rarely frequent them like to know that they are there, open and waiting, just in case. Recently, when I was preparing to conduct a memorial service for a neighbor who was not a member of the parish, I asked her husband if he would like to walk through the nave with me just to get a feel of the space, he replied, "Oh, no. I don't need to. I come in often when the church is open just to sit for a while. Our family doesn't belong, but we feel that it's our church."

This is not an isolated case: holy spaces invite us to drop in for a visit. When I lived in New York, I found myself arriving early for dental appointments so that I could sit for a while in the exotic, almost gaudy beauty of the immense Croatian church across from his office—not to steel myself for time with my gentle and competent dentist, but just to be for a little while in that spot where so many prayers of so many had soaked into the walls. Now and then I muse about the future of that building now that the neighborhood has changed: the hard-working, not-quite-assimilated children of immigrants are dying out, to be replaced by equally hard-working young people of quite different values. I suspect that even if the building is deconsecrated—which is often the fate of "redundant" churches—and turned into a club, it will still be a "thin" place. The writer of the letter to the Hebrews assures us that we are surrounded by a great cloud of witnesses, and that is no doubt what I felt. Some of the witnesses were aging men and women slipping in to say a prayer or two. Others I could not see, but I knew they were there; it was their prayers that had soaked into the building. It was they who kept me company while I loitered in their space.

I felt this the other day at St. Columba's, early in the morning before the service, when for the first time I noticed two small windows, set high in the chapel wall and scarcely noticeable. They were dedicated respectively to Mary Margaret and Amelia Ann Mulligan. There was no date, nothing else. The windows must have been placed there in 1926 when the building was new, but who were Mary Margaret and Amelia Ann? Were they respectable but probably formidable spinster sisters who gave generously of their time and substance but terrorized the rector? Or were they little girls who died of diphtheria, now a forgotten plague but a scourge of children some eighty years ago? I'll never know, but from now on I will welcome their companionship among all the other witnesses who hover there.

We need the comfort of each other to mark the milestones of our lives: the invisible, unknown cloud of witnesses who inhabit our sacred spaces, but also the flesh-and-blood company of others. Even those who do not know what they believe are drawn to mark important moments with ritual. As someone who loiters around a beautiful but not spectacular church in the midst of one of the busiest cities in the world, a city where power is wielded sometimes compassionately and sometimes ruthlessly, I am struck by the attraction of our modest stone building, just a short block off a busy street. If you do not notice the attached king-sized parish hall, it has the look of a comfortably weathered country church shaded by a giant oak. For the regulars it is a homely, homey place, where we find our friends, where we perhaps squabble a little now and then, where we go to pray and be prayed for. But like my neighbor who liked to come and sit now and then when no one was around, it is claimed by others who are drawn to its sustaining presence at crucial times, who recognize their need to hang out for a little with the great cloud of witnesses even if they don't quite believe in them.

At one time it was part of my job description to make referrals for people seeking spiritual direction. These were almost always thoughtful, sincere seekers: they had read books, gone through psychotherapy, practiced all kinds of meditation, and now they knew that they urgently wanted and needed something more. At some point in the interview, I would ask the crucial question: What is your faith community? With whom do you pray? For me it was a decisive question, since I could not in conscience suggest that someone embark alone on the journey of spiritual self-exploration. Typically I would hear something like "I'm spiritual, but not religious." Inevitably, the seeker was disappointed when I suggested that she find a community of praying people—all denominations welcome—and become part of the family, then come back and talk with me later. It was such a come-down for them to be directed to live among the ordinary and the fallible, the irritating and the downright stupid, the unenlightened and the self-satisfied. It did not help if I pointed out that the disciples themselves were just as limited a crew, but Jesus still found time for them. Like it or not, we all need our common ground.

We need the comfort of each other. We need it in ordinary times, but even more in threshold times when we celebrate or grieve, rejoice or despair. The rituals sustain us when we have no words. We take comfort in Benedictine stability even if we have never visited a monastery or heard of Benedict. Very few of us—maybe none?—have lived in the same house all our lives. We have fixed addresses, but there is always something provisional about them. As people of our time and place, we are on the move in ways great and small. Yet as we noted earlier, Benedict is adamant that the vow of stability—*stabilitas*—must be primary, and was highly critical of those who did not meet his standard.

The *sarabites,* for example, lived in small groups and did what they liked, rather like the free-wheeling student communes of the 1970s. Benedict had no kind words for the *gyrovagues,* who were constantly on the move from one monastery to another. I think I have met them in our own day, although they do not travel under that exotic name now; like the hummingbirds who frequent my overgrown garden, they flit from spiritual flower to flower. Finally there are the *cenobites,* those who live and flourish under the Rule. Perhaps that is who we can aspire to be: people deeply rooted, grounded in God, stable in times of grief and celebration no matter what the outward circumstances of our lives might be.

❖ *Anchored in Community*

A thoughtful rule demands that we seek the spiritual balance that can be found in the companionship of others. Companions, after all, are those with whom we share bread. In a worshiping community we share more than that: mutual accountability and support, but perhaps most importantly the sustenance that comes from being part of the great cloud of witnesses—past, present, and future. Far from restricting us, discovering and embracing the inner stability of the Benedictine spirit sets us free to live prayerfully and intentionally, to escape the confusion and dissonance of a society that offers us too much of nearly everything, good and bad, helpful and harmful. We are anchored instead of drifting aimlessly. We find it when we are gathered together on common ground. Fashions in liturgical music come and go, the ancient words of the tradition are updated and expanded, disagreements significant and trivial threaten our unity, but the church remains for many of us the best place to find our common ground.

There is the danger, of course, that we can make that fallible institution the object of idolatrous devotion. That is why it can be a beneficial exercise for liturgically centered Episcopalians to experience worship now and then with Baptists—who manage to pray without a book and who do not feel obliged to use the same words every Sunday. Or for sermon-focused Presbyterians to enjoy a bit of high Anglo-Catholic worship with incense and the most lavish vestments available. Or for time-obsessed North Americans to experience church as Sub-Saharan Africans know it. I shall never forget a ninety-minute sermon preached by a visiting Sudanese bishop in New York—it was a true learning experience and probably did us a world of good.

There is also the danger that we will try to turn the church into a museum of good taste, open only to card-carrying members. Then we can occupy ourselves with scaring away the undesirables or with welcoming newcomers so vociferously that they flee, never to return. I rejoice that my neighbor felt welcome just to come and sit without having to explain himself or sign a card or maybe risk a visit from the clergy that he did not want. I rejoice too that the worshipers in my beautiful Croatian church paid no attention to me, but got on with their own praying—not because they were ignoring me, but because they knew that for at least a little while, it was my church too. We can get carried away in our zeal to welcome the stranger, who perhaps is just passing through or who simply wants to test the spiritual waters before plunging in.

Those of us who find our rest and strength in church congregations must not forget and neglect those people for whom the church—for whatever reason—is not a sanctuary. In the liturgy for Good Friday we pray for "those who in the name of Christ have persecuted others." While most of us well-intentioned folk have not participated in anything on the scale of the Spanish Inquisition or the Crusades, we dare not lose sight that there are many who have been hurt by the church. Many have received judgment when they thirsted for mercy and have been ignored when they desperately needed to be embraced. To repair the damage, sometimes the damage of a lifetime, is slow and tender work. I remember myself as a young sojourner in a Europe where many regarded Americans as loud, brash, ill-mannered, and too rich for their own good. "You're very nice for an American" was a "compliment" I heard more than once. There's a lesson here for our parishes: even those who for whom churchgoing is difficult or at least ambiguous might, if they are lovingly received, decide that we are "very nice for a church."

I have written earlier about the parish where I am anchored today. When I returned to it after a nearly twenty-year absence, I remarked to the rector as we walked through the nave, "This is where we'll have my funeral." I could feel him pull back and realized that he was wondering what the mental or physical health of this newcomer might be. I reassured him that I was in no hurry, but knew that I had arrived home to a safe place.

Yet that Benedictine *stabilitas* is not restricted to one spot. I know that I am home whenever I am with my Christian friends in Hong Kong, where Taizé chants sound just the same when sung in Cantonese. I am home when I worship at the Marienkirche in Munich, or join my English friend Janet at her local church, which looks like something out of *Masterpiece Theater*. (I am sure that I saw

Miss Marple there one Sunday.) I knew that I was home not long ago when a small group of us celebrated the Eucharist on a Delaware beach at twilight on an early spring day—it was growing dark, the air was chilly, and we made a little altar of some stones in the sand. (Afterwards we laughed: would summer beachgoers know that they were lounging on holy ground?) I knew that I was home when I celebrated the Eucharist with my friend Marie as she lay dying. We made a little circle around her hospice bed, shared the bread and wine, and rejoiced in the comfort of each other. We were standing on common ground.

Questions for Prayer and Pondering

❖   Identify your "thin" times and places. What has been holy ground for you? If you cannot think of any such places, pledge yourself to greater attentiveness.

❖   Who are your saints? They may be people of faith who have molded your life by their prayers and example—perhaps a grandparent, a teacher, or a wise friend. They may be voices that speak to you from books ancient and modern—Dietrich Bonhoeffer, Thomas Merton, Gandhi, Simone Weil, Mary Oliver, or Gerard Manley Hopkins. How have these saints shaped your life in God?

❖   What is the place of ritual and worship in your life? Do you gather regularly with one community, or with several? As you contemplate this portion of your rule, ponder why and how you do what you do.

Body and Soul

Nestled discreetly among the greenery in my office at St. Columba's is a chalice. From the visitor's chair it looks like a simple blue-gray piece of pottery, designed for use as a eucharistic vessel; it is only when you look at it closely that you see the nude women circled around it. Some are tall and some short, some slim and some plump—what my mother would call "fleshy." They are holding hands and dancing. The chalice was a gift to me from a young friend who probably thought the room could do with a little spicing up. It would not occur to me to use it in a church service, not even one of the New Age and slightly heretical rituals that happen now and then. But I love to have it near me, where I can glance over from my chair and take in its playful joy in celebrating the human body, naked and undisguised.

Like it or not, we are embodied. Whether we glorify our bodies or maltreat them, whether we are obsessed with physical perfection or oblivious to our bulges and sags, we are our bodies. We are not souls inhabiting disposable, unimportant, unworthy containers. Our bodies are us.

The Bible tells us that the Word became flesh—a word that may make us uneasy, perhaps even uncomfortable. Flesh is soft, yielding, passive. Flesh receives; flesh can be done unto. It would not be at all the same if John's gospel read, "And the Word became skin and bones" or "a well-toned body" or even "an intricate nervous system." Instead, the Word became *flesh*—a marvelous, complicated, vulnerable, beautiful body. If we accept this truth, then our physical selves are to be cherished and celebrated. Yet as we sit in our less-than-perfect bodies and ponder this bit of gospel, we may be thinking, "Surely not me. Maybe Tiger Woods or Kate Moss or Jane Fonda, but not me." And the answer comes: "Yes, even you."

Throughout the centuries Christianity has not always lived into the truth of this, but rather has denied the body, punishing it because it was seen as unclean. I learned this when I was very young. I attended my little neighborhood school, which was barely large enough to be viable had its ranks not been swelled by the orphan residents of a "home" operated by a rigid, joyless Christian sect. There it was a foundational rule that bodies were a source of danger and had to be concealed, so the girls were almost as completely covered as religious Muslim women—no head scarves, but long sleeves and long, thick brown stockings even in the hottest weather. The bolder orphans rolled their stockings down to their ankles when they arrived at school and rolled them back up at the end of the day. Woe betide the ones who were apprehended; bodies needed to be punished as well as concealed. Sister Hull, a fierce little woman in a black bonnet, ran a taut ship and dealt ruthlessly with physical beauty.

I remember the day a new orphan arrived in our third-grade class. She was a lovely child with thick yellow braids. As a group the orphans were not quite acceptable as playmates, but the newcomer—her name is long gone from my memory—was instantly welcomed and courted because she was prettier than any of us. But the very next day, she arrived with close-cropped hair, almost like the women in World War II who were shorn because of their collaboration with the enemy. She cried quietly at her desk all day, but as the days went on she seemed to settle into the grim life at the Mission. In school, she relapsed into her own dreary social level and was no longer courted.

Such grim denial of the wonder of our bodies questions the goodness of creation, when the LORD studied his handiwork and pronounced it very good. Then, to make sure that his work continued, God commanded our first parents to be fruitful and to multiply, which would seem a command to enjoy the pleasures of their bodies. In the Hebrew Scriptures, children are a blessing: "Your wife shall be like a fruitful vine within your house, your children like olive shoots round about your table" (Psalm 128:3). It was the greatest blessing of all to dwell under one's own vine and fig tree, to plant vineyards and to eat their fruit—a life of physical comfort, of bodies honored and well cared for.

There were, of course, in Jesus' time and before, those religious sects who denied their bodies and engaged in harsh ascetical practices. From the earliest times the belief that the body is a shameful and distracting encumbrance to living a "spiritual life" has been a discordant strand woven into the fabric of our tradition. In this view the body is to be constrained and punished, like a lawless and incontinent dog at the other end of the leash. At the very least, since we cannot get rid of them altogether, our bodies should be ignored. This negative stance toward our bodies often affects us in subtle or unrecognized ways. We try to pretend that they are not there, or that we have never seen them before and are certainly not attached to them in any way.

This extreme view of holiness ignores the fact that Jesus came to us in a body. He ate and drank with pleasure and told stories filled with the imagery of feasting. He must have known from his own experience of hunger that those thousands of people gathered on the hillside to hear him teach were getting hungry by the end of the day, probably developing headaches and turning cranky, when he instructed his disciples to find them something to eat. And he must have known something about rapidly growing adolescent bodies when he healed Jairus's daughter: as soon as it was clear that she was indeed not dead but sleeping, he told her parents: "Get her something to eat." Unlike our own physicians, he touched people in order to heal them without putting on sterile gloves first.

❖ *Cherishing Our Bodies*
It is a necessary part of a rule of life to cherish our bodies, care for them, and see the beauty in their intricate design. But too often, most of us—men and women both—come to dislike them as the years pass, or at the very least to feel that they need major remodeling. The standards of others are ever before us: we are invited to "sculpt" our bodies by plastic surgery or "build" them into temples of musculature of comic book proportions. We fight to stave off aging or at least to disguise it. Yet in his first letter to the Corinthians, Paul reminds us of the sanctity of the body:

> Or do you not know that your body is a temple of the Holy Spirit within you, which you have from God, and that you are not your own? For you were bought with a price; therefore glorify God in your body. (1 Corinthians 6:19–20)

Paul happened to be railing against fornication at this point, but his words strike home: our bodies are holy, and they are on loan. For that matter, so are we.

That means we are expected to treat our bodies with at least as much loving care as we bring to our Lamborghini or our prizewinning Russian wolfhound. We need to recognize their beauty in all ages and shapes. I am sometimes tempted to emigrate to Hong Kong, where my younger Chinese friends realize that aging is beautiful and do not hesitate to tell me so. Indeed, from their perspective I am likely to get more beautiful with each passing year! When I am with them I am tempted to lie about my age—and add on a few years.

So what is our responsibility for our bodies? How do we care for them, honor and celebrate them? How do we accept their vulnerability and—ultimately—their mortality? A rule of life is more than a fitness regimen, but concern for our physical selves is nevertheless an important part. Here, as elsewhere, the ghosts of my farming forebears seem to be peering over my shoulder as I write, wondering what all the fuss is about. Our preoccupation with diet and exercise would have been an unimagined luxury. They ate what was available, the fruit of the land and their own labor. Too much sugar and other highly refined carbohydrates was scarcely a possibility. Nor did obesity and lack of exercise pose a problem: hard manual labor took care of that. A life without all our delightful and tempting choices must have been austere, but it came with its own built-in, fairly inflexible rule. Preventive medicine or vitamins or life-saving drugs were unknown. Surgery was risky business. The frail died. A sturdy body was a condition for survival.

What do we eat, when, and how much? Unlike those folk living in other times and places, it is possible for us to eat until we become literal mountains of flesh, unable to move. It is also possible to starve ourselves to death. We can enjoy the pleasant stimulation of a cup of coffee or a glass of wine, or we can poison ourselves with caffeine or alcohol. I have noticed that the purple prose of menus and restaurant reviews reserves the word "sinful" to describe desserts that are heavily laden with butter, sugar, and chocolate. That may be as close to really lurid sin as some of us come, but even the accompanying guilt is rather pleasant. On the other hand, we can also become austerely abstemious and enjoy the pleasure of judging others' self-indulgence, which is often more fun than indulging ourselves.

How hard do we work our bodies? It takes very little physical energy to tap away at the computer keyboard. I think that I am tired at the end of the day, but if I bother to listen to my body, it's saying, "Get up and get moving.

Maybe your brain and fingers think that they're tired, but the rest of you hasn't moved all day. A computer potato is just as pathetic as a couch potato." Alas, my Nordic Trac is dusty, but I am filled with good intentions. Maybe next week ... or next month ... or maybe never. On the other hand, I comfort myself with the fact that I am a walker and a runner—up and down flights of stairs, wherever I find them. Our bodies must be used: big muscles must contract and relax, our hearts have to be pushed to beat a little faster, if we are to cherish them.

Good rules are freely chosen. I cannot open my morning paper nowadays without being assaulted by cautionary articles about obesity epidemics in our elementary schools, the hazards of sagging bodies and slack muscles after thirty, and dire predictions of whatever (I hate to think) is taking up residence in my own arteries. But instead of being motivated, I confess that scolding or scaring—even the impersonal chiding from the printed page—does not bring out the best in me. I even get a tad obstinate, as I mutter to myself that I am still breathing, indeed feel pretty good, so what's the problem? It occurs to me that I am not alone in this reaction. Care of our bodies is, after all, a work of love, to be undertaken with joy.

My Scottish grandfather never saw a doctor in his life. Nor, so far as I know, did he take any medications, not even an occasional aspirin. He just got on with his life: he managed his grocery store until he retired to plant his garden and tend the chickens, ate heartily enough, slept soundly for about eight hours every night, wore long underwear in the winter, read the newspaper every day, and avoided conflict. He died at eighty, right after he finished mowing the lawn, a good if unthinking steward of his body. Times have changed. No matter how good our inherited DNA, prudence demands more attentiveness to the physical self as part of a rule of life.

Right alongside exercise, the question of our physical work, comes the issue of rest. We drive ourselves so hard these days! I remember my time in graduate school, when I allowed myself six hours of sleep with just a little extra on Sundays. Now I have forgotten most of what I crammed into my head in those years of asceticism that rivaled the body-mortifying practices of the desert fathers. At the time it felt intellectually heroic, but now it looks a bit foolish. When our bodies need sleep, we should let them sleep.

True rest, however, is much more than getting adequate sleep. If we are to enjoy true rest, we must understand the spirit of the Sabbath. It is not enough merely to cease working; we need to celebrate the gift of refreshing time and space. So ask yourself, "What makes me new? What re-creates me?" I am re-created by movies...books...just sitting by the Hazel River and watching the water swirl over the stones. Sometimes I am made new by a brisk walk, as fast as I can go. Almost always I am made new by hanging out for a while with my grandchildren Jack and Sam, nine and six respectively, who generously welcome me into their world. Ongoing association with children, who live closer to the ground than I do, is a powerful restorative. For all of us recreation—which is really re-creation—is a highly individual matter and very much a part of a liveable rule of life. There are so many possibilities: study, manual labor, sport, exercise, writing, painting, building, enjoying the beauty created by others in images and words, solitude, conversation, and company—to name just a few. To see our way of recreation as vital to our well-being, as necessary as sleep and exercise, is not self-indulgence but self-preservation.

Children and other small animals—especially cats—are much better at this than most of us. They usually know when they are tired, and they simply let go. I am filled with admiration for our parish babies who just go limp when they have had enough, sound asleep in their elegant strollers or Snugglis, or slung over a parental shoulder. To be sure, they don't have elaborate "to-do" lists in their still-developing brains, nor do they carry BlackBerry Devices or Palm Pilots. Yet even making those adjustments, they could teach us a lot about recognizing the necessity—and the joy—of true rest and holy uselessness.

❖ A Community of Embodied Creatures

We are called to honor not only our own bodies, but the bodies of others as well. As embodied creatures, we are sexual beings who, according to the creation story, are not meant to be alone. But sexuality at any age can be hard to navigate. Communities ponder what to do about their "registered sex offenders": label them for life or let them blend into the neighborhood, in the hope that they have seen the error of their ways? As one working in a parish setting, I take obligatory courses about "boundary violations," in which I am tutored in "acceptable areas of touch." The Internet offers me the opportunities to explore aspects of human behavior that would have my parents spinning in their graves. Even the annoying Spam, which intrudes itself into my benign e-mail correspondence, suggests that there are a lot of titillating things out there that I still need to know, even after almost fifty years of marriage and the birth of three children. I feel out-of-step in my society, but I comfort myself with the thought that Adam and Eve, enjoying Eden in their uninhibited innocence before the Fall, would feel out-of-step, too.

Oddly enough, I find myself very aware of bodies when we baptize new Christians at church. I say "oddly" because—as contrasted with those earliest days of the church, when the adult candidates were immersed naked in cold, running water—everyone in our services is fully clothed. The physical aspect of the rite has been reduced to a sprinkling of lukewarm water on the head and a signing of the cross on the candidate's forehead. Still, the babies are the most embodied—and the easiest. Soft and cuddly, they nestle in my arms, and some of the truly laid-back manage to sleep through their transition from heathen to

Christian. Even disguised in a voluminous ancestral chris-
tening dress, their bodies are new, beautiful, and a glimpse
of the wonder of creation. The bigger children are something else: the bodies are still beautiful, but they are strong
and energetic, shy or spunky, all full of promise. They can
fight back—which they sometimes do. And then there are
the adults. When I place my hand on a shoulder to guide
someone toward the font, or when I sign his or her forehead with the cross, I am conscious of the body as well as
the soul. Each is a whole person, a totality, made in God's
image—tall and short, fat and thin, all sorts of skin colors,
some brand-new and others quite shopworn.

The baptismal font is much bigger than the chalice in
my office, but it isn't nearly big enough to capture the
great circle dance of bodies celebrated at baptism, a joyous
reversal of the grim medieval pictures of the Dance of
Death. Yes, we are mortal. Yes, our bodies eventually wear
out or succumb to illness or injury. But Sister Hull, who
once stalked out of a PTA gathering where the program
featured nine-year-old Jeannie Kirkpatrick tap-dancing,
hadn't caught on. She missed the point: our bodies are
made for dancing, and they are all beautiful, clothed or
unclothed.

Like the potter who created my circle of dancing
women, I would like to create a much bigger chalice and
cover it with figures: frail octogenarian Jenny with her
walker, reaching down to hold the hand of my three-year-
old friend Alec, to whom dancing comes naturally—he'll
learn to walk later. Nearby I would add a few utterly gor-
geous teenagers and maybe a few scruffy ones who have
shaved their heads or could use a haircut. Then there's
Cathy, a Down syndrome child who lights up a room
when she enters it, next to a stately bishop or two in full
regalia and some homeless folk, too, and Charlie, whose
stroke has left him off-balance and shuffling but who
always has a joke for anyone who stops to listen. All around
the rim of my enormous chalice I would place my chic

young mother friends who never have a hair out of place, and all my non-chic friends who do. My friend Millie, who's built like a refrigerator, beside my friend Greg, whose good looks and perfect body would put a Banana Republic male model to shame. All those bodies, a nice assortment of races and ethnicities, shapes and sizes. All made in the image of God.

Questions for Prayer and Pondering

❖　In the privacy of your bathroom or bedroom, take a good look at your body. Where do you see beauty? Strength? Where do you feel called to say, "Forgive me. I will try to take better care of you"? Where do you feel called to say, "Thank you, faithful friend"?

❖　What bodily care or attention needs to be added to your rule of life? Where have you been neglectful in caring for your body? Where and how have you failed to celebrate and cherish it?

❖　How do we come to accept our body's mortality? In what ways have you had to come to terms with the limitations of your body? with aging?

❖　In what ways do you honor and cherish the bodies of other people?

Lifelong Learning

I was fifty years old when I began the study of theology to pursue what is graciously called a "mature vocation" to the priesthood. Up to that time, my life had been spent in one corner of academe or another, first in years of study culminating in a Ph.D. in Germanic languages and literature, then in all sorts of teaching situations. I could not wait for the thrill and challenge of exploring a new discipline. I read the catalog eagerly, in the same spirit in which I read gourmet cookbooks. I anticipated a rich feast—yet this time instead of feeding others, I would be fed.

On the first day of a foundational Scripture course, the professor distributed a bulky syllabus along with many tips on how to study. Instead of resenting her condescension, I became anxious: maybe I didn't really know how to go about the work of learning despite all those years in library stacks. There were extensive lists for the absolutely required reading and equally long lists for the strongly recommended. Since there was even an assignment for the first day of class, which we theological neophytes had not known about, we were already behind when we entered the classroom! What made the biggest impression, however, was a detailed half-page explaining the penalties for late work:

grade points would be steadily deducted for each day of delinquency until suicide was the only option. I was stunned, and although for the most part the three years that followed were indeed a rich feast, I never forgot my bafflement and outrage that the adventure of learning was presented as drudgery motivated by threats. Despite the unexpected blow on that first day of new beginnings, my zest for study and learning was alive and well, perhaps stronger than ever, and I was grateful for the privilege of beginning again, adding another layer to my life in academe.

Curiositas, the Latin ancestor of our word "curiosity," is the pursuit of learning narrowly for its own sake and to the neglect of deeper purpose. The early church saw it as a dangerous distraction because it diverted the seeker from the Christian's true purpose, which was to grow in the knowledge and love of God. Both Aquinas and Augustine regarded overzealous devotion to study as an impediment, but the holy men of the Egyptian desert were even more drastic. "Get rid of your books," counsels Abba Macarius. "Sell them, and give the money to the poor. It is best of all to possess nothing." Abba Moses was even more direct when he commanded his disciples: "Go, sit in your cell, and your cell will teach you everything." I think about him when I sit in my comfortable twenty-first-century version of a cell, surrounded by books, the Internet at my fingertips. I can see the possibility of falling into the sin of gluttony by amassing data instead of focusing on deep learning, and amassing books the way my grandsons pile up Legos. Just as we have been told we can never be too rich or too thin, I persuade myself that we can never have too many books. There's always room for just a few more, especially if you stack them two deep.

❖ *Inquiring and Discerning Hearts*

What part does lifelong learning play in a rule of life? First of all we have to realize that learning is more than piling up books, calculating the tens of thousands of pages we

have read, and accumulating data. I regret that a prayer for
the gifts of the Holy Spirit, which is said over the newly
baptized and after that forgotten about, is not imprinted
more deeply on our consciousness:

> Sustain them, O Lord, in your Holy Spirit. Give them an
> inquiring and discerning heart, the courage to will and to
> persevere, a spirit to know and to love you, and the gift
> of joy and wonder in all your works. (BCP, 308)

Although we share our opposable thumbs with other pri-
mates, our inquiring minds and discerning hearts, accompanied by the tools of language and memory, are part of
what it means to be made in the image of God.

We are expected to use these gifts in the service of
God, to know and to love God, and in our own growth
and development, to know and to love ourselves. It is
temptingly easy, however, to turn off our minds and dis-
connect our good sense when we move from workaday to
spiritual concerns. It is tempting to remain stuck in child-
ish understandings of God and immature theological
beliefs, and to feel that the work of learning is done once
we have graduated from confirmation class, if we ever
went at all. How easy it is to shrink from risk, to let our
hearts and minds grow small and constricted instead of
bold and expansive. People of faith who are well informed
about economics, philosophy, political affairs, and the arts
and sciences can be all too willing to turn their minds off
when their faith is involved. Perhaps we fear that our fee-
ble construct of God cannot bear the impact of critical
thinking.

But Benedict, unlike his holy forebears of the desert,
reminds us that any split between mind and soul is a false
dichotomy; our intellects are an integral part of our spirituality. As such, they deserve a share of our time and our
energy long after we have completed our formal education. "Idleness," he tells us, "is the enemy of the soul.
Therefore the brethren should be occupied at certain

times with manual labor, and again at fixed hours in sacred reading" (chp. 48). Most of our labor nowadays isn't manual, but we are still a work-obsessed people. Study, however, is another matter: we live in the mistaken belief that it is the province of the young. I was home-schooled for a year, long before the term was ever coined. My mother had no training as a teacher, but I was so eager to learn that we figured it out as we went along. Reading simply happened—we had my brother's old books, which I read to her while she worked her way through a pile of ironing. From a kindergarten teacher friend, she hit on the idea of printing one word on a 3 x 5 card, which turned into a lot of words on a great pile of cards. From these I would make stories on the floor, starting in the living room, running through the dining room and ending in the little sewing room, where I would run out of space and cards. For writing, I was allowed to use the family typewriter. It was one of the first hardships of my young life when I learned that I would have to know at least how to print my letters with a pencil.

Real school was another story. When I entered second grade after reluctantly demonstrating my prowess with a Number 2 pencil, our chief task in arithmetic was to master what the teacher called "combinations"—one plus one equals two, one plus two equals three, and so on up to ten plus ten equals twenty. We were expected to write the series of little sums over and over, acres of them, until they were permanently etched in our brains. I soon learned that the whole operation went more quickly if I wrote a whole line of ones and beneath them the sequence of numbers up to ten, preceded by a plus sign; then beneath each pair of digits a neat little line; and finally the sum. And so on through the whole exercise. Miss Shannon never noticed my method, but praised my neatness and speed. Now I wonder if my present mathematical disability might have been avoided if somehow I had been made aware of the mystery and promise of numbers, a gift that had come to me naturally with words. At any rate, there was little joy and wonder as I filled page after page with ones and twos.

Of course we need to learn the basics, which are not always interesting and whose usefulness must be taken on faith. This is especially true when our faith demands that we learn to think theologically. This may send us into a kind of panic—even as we yearn to learn more and more about our faith, we may despair of our ability to contort our brains into new possibilities. Learning to think theologically is different from the learning required to gain moderate proficiency in a new language, which many of us have already managed to do adequately, if not brilliantly. Theology affects our deepest thoughts and yearnings, and we may fear that our very identity might be called into question if we delve too deeply in learning about our faith. Now I realize that *all* our serious thinking should be theological, because all knowledge is part of the mind of the God who created all that is. Even if we are unable to skate comfortably amid words like *epistemology* and *soteriology,* to say nothing of *hermeneutic,* we are all capable of learning more about our faith in God. Although useful, the arcane vocabulary can be a smoke screen, and it is reassuring to remember that Jesus' vocabulary was straightforward and deceptively simple.

❖ *God's Curriculum*

So what do we study? If our aim is to apply our inquiring minds and discerning hearts to all God's works, the curriculum is vast. The book of nature is all around us. Here there can be no end to our learning, whether we are fascinated by the blight on the backyard rose bushes or the currents of the tsunami, the circulation of our blood or the exploration of space. The study of all the sciences is ultimately theological study, whether we are amateur or professional. And amateur status is not to be discounted, since the amateur is a lover who learns for the love of learning.

A fascination with words has dominated my own life of study. I still remember my excitement in my ninth-grade Latin class, which was my first encounter with a foreign language, other than bits of German learned from my father. The laborious translations and rote memorization should have been tedious, but I was enthralled by the prospect of learning unfamiliar words for such familiar things. At about the same time, I fell in love with my native English and was obnoxious in my zeal to weave my new discoveries into my homework. I still recall my satisfaction when I could finally fit "unambiguously" into a book report!

And, of course, words knit together made stories. Although I could not have articulated it when I was young, I perceived everything as a story, as narrative. Not only literature, but history, psychology, and—to my delight and surprise—even theology could be seen as part of a story. It is no accident that Jesus is Logos, the Word, and that the Bible is our big family storybook. Every now and then, if someone calls me a "theologian," I wince and try to clarify: "No, I just like stories. I like to pick words apart and push them back to their beginnings, then see how they all come together again." As I reflect now, there has been a graced coherence in my lifetime of learning: eventually everything comes together, like pieces of an intricate mosaic that will never be quite finished. This is indeed the work of a lifetime.

Abba Macarius instructed Abba Pherme to dispose of his books. He had only three, yet that was apparently enough to distract him from his life of prayer. By contrast, we have an abundance of avenues to learning: books, journals, film, lectures, tapes, and CD-ROMs—not to mention our eyes and ears. Augustine, Benedict, and our other monastic ancestors who valued learning lived before the information explosion. There could be no danger of excess or superficiality in their way of study. A monk read slowly and ruminated on what was read; then he probably went back and read it again. And again. It can be no accident that this very agricultural verb is used to describe monastic study: like meditative cows slowly chewing and chewing until they have got the last bit of nourishment from their mouthful of grass, the ruminant reader is in no hurry. That is how I read stories and was read to as a child, no doubt because children back then were not inundated with books. The faithful few on my shelf became old friends, to be visited regularly until I knew them by memory.

This practice proved to be useful when, as an adult, I needed to teach myself Spanish. I was not aiming for elegance or eloquence, just enough for survival. I had studied grammar diligently, but now the enterprise needed to be brought to life. I was overjoyed when I found a paperback translation of Louisa May Alcott's *Little Women* on a Mexico City pushcart. I knew then that I had found my way home on the very first page: *"'Es muy triste decirlo, pero somos pobres,' mumuro Meg."* ("'It's so dreadful to be poor,' sighed Meg.") I had read, marked, learned, and inwardly digested *Little Women* when I was seven years old with a thoroughness that would have made Benedict proud. I moved triumphantly through *Mujercitas,* then returned to my pushcart source and picked up *Anne of Green Gables—Ana de los Tejados Verdes*—followed by *Las Aventuras de Sherlock Holmes.* By the time I had gone through my new little library at least twice, I could carry on comfortable if untidy conversations in my new language.

At the time I didn't assign a deeper significance to those weeks of reading; I simply saw my method as a rather pleasurable and effective means to an end. Upon reflection, however, I realized that I had so immersed myself in my childhood favorites that the words and sentences were almost a part of me. Now I was seeing them with new eyes; they had lost nothing, indeed had taken on a new texture. Gradually it has occurred to me that over the years I have read Scripture in the same way—sometimes in German or Spanish, just for the linguistic adventure, sometimes in the *King James Version* of the Bible of my childhood, most often nowadays in the *New Revised Standard Version*. We do not gallop through the sixty-six books of Holy Writ (not counting the Apocrypha) with the sense of instant mastery: "Great! Now I've done it! Now I can get on to something else." No, our engagement with Scripture is another work of a lifetime: we immerse ourselves, let ourselves sink deeper and deeper through layers of meaning, let the words become almost a part of our own skin.

There is so much to learn, and just to keep abreast of current events is an impossible task, even when we fall back on the quick fix of television news or magazine reporting. There is so much to know and to begin to understand that our brains are reeling. Yet the kind of study that Benedict prescribes demands that we apply our minds as well as our emotions to our relationship not only with God, but all that God has made. At times I am tempted to turn off my thought processes, to persuade myself that trying to understand what is happening in the Middle East and Korea, South Africa, and our inner cities, the Amazon rain forest and the pharmaceutical industry has nothing to do with my identity in Christ. Life would be easier if empathy with human and environmental distress were sufficient, but it's not. Action is required.

Perhaps even more important is the application of our intellect to our faith. It may be disturbing to bring a certain rigor and discipline to the study of Scripture, to wrestle with its inconsistencies and let our old certainties be challenged. The good news here is that God is strong enough to withstand our poking and prodding, maybe even delights in it as a loving parent enjoys being poked and prodded by that inquisitive toddler who likes to push buttons. An unexamined faith is a dangerous faith: false gods are all around us, alive and alluring. When we think that we have God all figured out and that we are infallible interpreters of God's will, we are in trouble.

If we live by a rule, the commitment to learning should be almost as important a part of our regimen as our commitment to prayer. It keeps us from remaining at a comfortable and undemanding level of spiritual immaturity. So we keep on learning—from books, from tradition, from the shared wisdom of our community, and from our own experience. If we wish to deepen our understanding of our faith there are so many options today: participating in an Education for Ministry (EFM) group or a class in our parish, finding a course at a local seminary or college, exploring online opportunities, or the good old-fashioned tried-and-true approach of thoughtful reading on our own. Above all, we must not be afraid to grapple with hard questions or to confront our uncertainties. The study of Scripture, theology, and church history is a rich feast to be embraced and enjoyed. Just as an unexamined life is not worth living, so an unexamined faith is not worth having.

Questions for Prayer and Pondering

❖   Where is the place for study in your rule of life?

❖   What areas of study do you need to revisit? Are there subjects that perhaps you have avoided or that were neglected in your years of formal education? What new field could you explore as a spiritual and intellectual adventure?

❖   Most simply: we learn by paying attention. What new thing have you learned today—not from a book, but from exercising your gift of joy and wonder in all God's works?

13

Work:
Promise and Peril

My farming forebears worked very hard just to scratch out a living. It probably never occurred to them to question why they labored since there were so few choices in a world where survival was the main task at hand. I often wonder how they would have identified themselves, if some inquisitive stranger had asked them who they really were. Since everyone of their acquaintance was a farmer or a farmer's wife, their daily hard work was not a distinguishing characteristic. So they might have claimed identity by location (we have the farm next to the Kurzweils') or kinship (I'm Henry Kunz's nephew) or ethnicity (we're from New England, not like those Germans who can't even speak the language) or maybe religion (Protestant, of course; Methodist to be exact).

I sometimes think about these folk when I find myself in a get-acquainted situation, one of those gatherings where you encounter people whom you will never meet again. How do you create a little sense of connection in this brief encounter? There are so many bits of information we might offer: I grew up in the Middle West. . . . I like to travel. . . . I like to read whodunits. . . . I used to bake bread but don't anymore. . . . I'm the mother of three children. . . . I'm an old movie addict. . . . I'm active in my church. But I have yet to encounter someone at one of those quasi-social gatherings who volunteers such bits of identity, either significant or trivial. Almost inevitably we identify ourselves—and others—by our work.

This is not a new phenomenon. Not long ago I entertained myself on a tedious flight just listing in my mind the English surnames that denote occupations, indeed some occupations no longer in existence. It became almost hypnotic: butcher, baker, fisher, farmer, carpenter, shoemaker, tailor, sailor, and on and on. Why did they need so many smiths? The fletchers made arrows, the chandlers made candles and soap, the fullers and dyers worked with cloth, the coopers made barrels—what a humble heritage for Gary Cooper, the heartthrob of my movie-going youth. I was still finding names when the plane touched down in Dallas.

In a sense, we _are_ our work. We are even identified by what we _don't_ do—the unemployed, the welfare recipient, and the homeless are nonworkers in a society where preoccupation with work approaches the idolatrous. Even worthy, essential occupations are relegated to a low status. I recall a time leading a contemplative retreat when I said, admittedly tongue-in-cheek, "After all, I'm just a housewife." My partner in the conversation was genuinely shocked: "Oh no, not you!" (She had apparently envisaged me moving gracefully all day between my private chapel and my splendid library—no raggedy paperbacks, everything leather-bound.) As I remembered that I had left a shockingly dirty kitchen floor at home and that a heap of laundry was awaiting me when I returned, I realized that what had been intended as irony was really quite true. Of course I am a housewife, and have been one for decades. It is as much a part of my identity as priest or writer or professor, all more elegant occupations than mopper of floors and washer of dishes.

❖ *The Value of Work*

We know from Scripture that we are expected to work, although Jesus was remarkably cavalier about calling fishermen from their nets and farmers from their plows. Paul is even tougher than usual when he writes to the Thessalonians: the idle are to be shunned, and those who refuse to work should not eat.

> For we hear that some of you are living in idleness, mere busybodies, not doing any work. Now such persons we command and exhort in the Lord Jesus Christ to do their work quietly and to earn their own living. Brothers and sisters, do not be weary in doing what is right. (2 Thessalonians 3:11–13)

Since in the Roman Empire any physical work was demeaning, tasks to be performed by slaves, the documents of early monasticism seek to redeem honest, humble labor. Out in the desert St. Antony worked with his hands, for he had heard that the lazy person did not deserve to eat. He grew his own food and earned a little money weaving baskets. One day, when he was at work, a demon arrived at his cell, a monstrous creature whom Antony immediately recognized as evil. He simply made the sign of the cross and said: "I am Christ's servant. If you are on a mission against me, here I am." But the monster with its demons fled so fast that its speed caused it to fall and die. Who knows what might have happened if Antony had just been sitting there woolgathering? Or if the Tempter had chosen a better disguise? To his soul's peril, Antony might have stopped working.

The medieval monastic rules are clear about the importance of humble, menial work—partly as a spiritual discipline but more practically because there is a certain amount of ongoing work in the community that must be done. So, with rare exceptions, Benedict excuses no one from regular kitchen duty. At the end of one week's rotation, the retiring kitchen worker cleans up the kitchen, washes "the towels with which the brethren wipes their hands and feet," and returns all kitchen implements clean and in good condition to the cellarer, who will issue them to the incoming server (chp. 35). I love this chapter of the Rule because it takes what has traditionally been woman's work seriously! It also spreads it around. Not only are we all expected to perform these humble tasks, but we are expected to clean up after ourselves. On those occasions when I am quartered in a hotel rather than a monastic house, I have to suppress my reflexes as I remind myself not to make the bed and not to tidy up the bathroom. If all guests embraced the importance and sanctity of such humble work, we would create unemployment in the housekeeping department, but it would probably be good for us.

❖ The Peril of Work

One of Benedict's claims to distinction is his elevation of work, menial work, to a high place in the human value system. His inclusion of manual labor as part of the Rule was a way of sanctifying the ordinary, of reminding us of the potential holiness of the material, that the work of our hands can be sanctified and approached in the spirit of God. In the sixth century, this new emphasis on work was important in the achievement of balance. But we are a people whose lives are out of balance. We can bring a self-punishing intensity to our work that rivals the austere practices of desert fathers! We do not talk much about the sin of idolatry these days—lust, adultery, and murder are more attractive to the media and appeal to the voyeur in us as well. But idolatry is alive and well, and perhaps the chief in the pantheon of false gods is Chronos, the voracious god of time who devoured his children.

It may require a dramatic disruption to restore a healthy perspective, one of those perceived losses that force us to look at ourselves and our lives with new eyes. My friend Joe, indefatigable in his service at the church's homeless shelter, can always tell me which new movie I must see. I had always admired him for his ability to devote himself passionately to whatever task was at hand, to love the sometimes difficult population whom he served in his volunteer ministry, while still having time to go to a movie. Then he told me his story: a near-fatal accident before he was fifty, when he was at the top of his profession and aiming to climb still higher, forced him to rethink *everything*. After a long and difficult recovery, he wondered how he should use his precious time and energy. He probably works harder now than he ever did in ascending the corporate ladder, but like Benedict's monks he has his priorities straight: his life is no longer centered around compulsive work, but around what really matters in God's great economy. Instead of draining him, his work nourishes him.

If we recognize and take seriously the concept of Sabbath, we will not succumb to the peril of work. Recognizing its necessity and even its potential holiness, we will keep it in its proper place. We will take seriously the command to rest—not grudgingly as a sign of weakness but as a necessary ingredient of good stewardship of our time and energy. We will look forward to Sabbath time, whichever day of the week it falls on for us. The LORD God was very clear when he laid down the law to the Israelites: not only do you stop working, but your children, your slaves, the sojourner in your community, and even your domestic animals get a day off. I find it difficult to let go of the burden of work, to set it down in confidence that everything will be right there when I am ready to pick it up again. I try to blame this on my ethnicity and upbringing—New Englanders and Germans are terribly serious people, and the Middle West of my early days was renowned for its tight embrace of the work ethic. Not one of my ancestors spent his days lounging in a hammock under a palm tree. But in my heart of hearts, I know that this is just an excuse and a loss of perspective.

❖ Holy Uselessness

In one of my classes I required the students to prepare a rule of life that would go beyond their devotional practices and spiritual disciplines and instead be broadly comprehensive, reflecting balance in all aspects of their daily lives. In other words, they were to create the sort of rule I am talking about here. They entered into the exercise enthusiastically and presented me with thoughtful and candid papers. They had examined their use of time and energy, reflected carefully on their relationship with those whose lives touched theirs (including the difficult and incompatible ones), scrutinized their performance as custodians of God's creation. All in all, it was exemplary work except for one thing: these were grim, dreary schedules that allowed no place for fun. No room for holy uselessness or the joyous and restorative wasting of time, a spiritual discipline that bears absolutely no resemblance to guilt-producing procrastination or avoidance of whatever the next step might be. If they were able to live out the plan that they laid out for themselves, they would be exemplary citizens, conscientious pray-ers, and ecologically beyond reproach. But they would never have any fun.

It was a happy day when I discovered that in the English of Chaucer's day—which was also the time of the Black Death—the word "silly" meant "blessed." I am not sure when we strayed away from its original meaning, when blessedness took on a churchy aura and silliness became the realm of Monty Python and fourth-grade scatological humor. As hard-working adults we too often lose the gift for letting go, for delight in simply *being*. We persuade ourselves that every moment must be lived productively; like the busy little bee, we feel a holy obligation to improve each shining hour. We would do well to take very small children or big silly dogs as our teachers. I have learned much about holy uselessness from Perry, the dog of undistinguished ancestry who lives down the road from me in Jenkins Hollow. He is never in a hurry. He savors the

Amen.

sunshine. He is tolerant of human imperfection. He is happiest when one of his human friends stops long enough to scratch his belly or that delicious, unreachable place behind his ears. In his comfortable canine way, he lives each day to the fullest.

From my window at church I am able to watch—sometimes with a tad of envy—the preschoolers cavorting on the playground. Intensely serious play can dissolve into uninhibited silliness in the twinkling of an eye. They are delightfully at home in their bodies. With an astonishing litheness they let themselves tumble headlong down the grassy hill in the full assurance that they will come to a halt before they crash into the big oak tree. (The winter version of this exercise involves sliding over the same snow-covered hill on large sheets of cardboard.) Unlike their shopworn elders, they do not need to be made new—they are already new! Instead there is a kind of joyous abandon in their play, which, quite appropriately, is the serious work of growing up.

Watching them forces me to contemplate the question: what makes me new? Is there a place for holy uselessness in my purposeful life? What re-creates me? It is high time that we reclaim this word, for recreation has become an industry. Its pursuit may demand special clothes, shoes, equipment; it may cost quite a lot of money; and we work hard—and often joylessly—at it. Re-creation is something else. No matter how tired and worn down we might feel, it makes us new. It merits an important place in our rule of life.

The possibilities are endless. One of my friends is refreshed and re-created by rigorous study. The very names of the theological courses that she takes at a nearby seminary frighten me in their austerity, but her eyes sparkle when she tells me about the paper she is writing or the arcane book she is plowing through. Jean runs several miles every day and pants out her intercessions rather than saying them. Tom is an old movie buff; his life has taken on new luster with the advent of the DVD. My retired dentist neighbor takes saxophone lessons. Sam, whose office job keeps him chained to a desk for fifty hours a week, spends Saturday afternoons coaching little kids in soccer, not from any sense of civic duty, but rather because he is able to see with new eyes and hear with new ears after several hours of running around a field with a pack of eight-year-olds. Some of us look for a good party with old friends, while others of us are drawn to solitude. The point, of course, is this: we forget about achievement, we forget about accomplishing obligatory tasks, we forget about pleasing others, and for a little while each day we emulate my preschool friends tumbling down the hill—in an adult way, of course.

Twenty-four hours spent listening to the river in Jenkins Hollow can make me new. Similarly, two hours with a movie—all the way from an old Bette Davis two-handkerchief drama to an obscure and gloomy German movie of the 1970s. Or a little while with one of Mary Oliver's poems. Or an hour at the cathedral, watching the play of sunlight through the stained-glass windows. Or immersing myself in one of Meister Eckhart's sermons, preferably in German.

❖ The Promise of Work

If we maintain a healthy balance, our work can be filled with promise. Much as we might look forward to unbroken leisure, meaningful work keeps us inwardly alive, alert, and ready for the next challenge, great or small. Antony in the desert was steadied and centered by his basket-weaving, which kept the demons at bay. Our demons are less recognizable than his, but steady, meaningful work can be emotionally and spiritually healing. We know that the great personal losses in our lives must be grieved, and we know that the processes must be allowed to move at their own slow pace. Yet real work, not mindless diversion, can be tremendously healing in a time of grief. Manual labor is restorative, and if its result brings help or solace to our neighbor, so much the better. We need to broaden our concept of occupational therapy! Repetitive, silent work can be a form of meditation. I try to remember this when I scrub that neglected kitchen floor. My whole body is involved, its movements are rhythmic, and my mind is emptied. This can be a contemplative exercise instead of a boring task. Unfortunately, helpful machines have made much work of this sort obsolete. Much as I love all my labor-saving devices, I can feel—mostly when I am in a sentimental mood—a twinge of regret for a time when we worked more with our hands and our bodies.

In many ways, we are formed by our work: a lifetime accretion of skills and knowledge, disappointments and happy surprises builds in us over the years and makes us who we are. I look back over the work I have done, most of it good and—even though I did not always perceive it at the time—worth doing. As a small girl I was charged with dusting the wicker furniture (a job I hated); I have been the reader of innumerable books and writer of forgettable term papers. As wife and mother I was the changer of ten thousand diapers, the cooker of meals and mopper of sticky floors—and the unlicensed practitioner of medicine, part of the job description of any mother. I am still a teacher of classes and preacher of sermons. And on and on, layer upon layer.

In *The Way of Perfection* Teresa of Avila prays: "Lord, you are to be blessed and praised; all good things come from you: you are in our words and in our thoughts, and in all that we do." It's a good prayer to ponder as we contemplate a rule of life: as good caretakers of our time and energy, how do we structure our days so that our work is a source of life and growth instead of a harmful, soul-deadening obsession? The work of our minds and hands can be a peril or a promise. The choice is ours.

Questions for Prayer and Pondering

❖   What is your work? Is it synonymous with your job? Is it a friend and companion, or a harsh and demanding enemy?

❖   How do you use work to keep the demons at bay? Have you dared to look at those demons up close and call them by name?

❖   Observance of the Sabbath is commanded, not suggested. What does your Sabbath look like? Where is the place for holy uselessness in your rule?

14

The Fear of Abundance

In Bernard Shaw's *Pygmalion* Alfred P. Doolittle, ne'er-do-well father of Eliza, demands five pounds from Professor Higgins in exchange for his daughter. Higgins, captivated by his outrageousness and his distinctive use of language, offers him ten. Doolittle replies, "No, Governor. Ten pounds is a lot of money: it makes a man feel prudent like; and then goodbye to happiness. You give me what I ask you, Governor: not a penny more, and not a penny less." Alfred P. Doolittle has grasped something that he can scarcely articulate. He recognized that possessing too much, instead of setting him free, would make him "feel prudent like." He would have to give up the carefree life of the grasshopper and emulate the conscientious ant. Abundance would bring with it the responsibility for stewardship. It might also bring with it fear or at least caution: five pounds could be spent quickly—probably on drink for himself, his missus, and his cronies—but ten pounds demanded care. If not disposed of quickly, it might be stolen or lost. Living meagerly, instead of abundantly, was safer. Or at least easier.

If abundance means having enough, more than enough, indeed possessing seemingly limitless resources, why should we fear it? Why might the awareness of our abundance leave us uneasy and unsatisfied? After all, Scripture is filled with the promise of abundance as the reward for faithfulness. Such bounty is not earned compensation, but a gift, lavishly bestowed by a generous God. The promised land flows with milk and honey, symbols of abundance. Those who honored the LORD with their substance were assured that their barns would be filled with plenty, and their vats bursting with wine.

Our twenty-first-century abundance looks quite different. Gold from Arabia and thick-growing grain are alien images in my corner of the world, yet I am overwhelmed every time I wander through the gourmet grocery on our shopping street. It is an aesthetic experience to contemplate the mountains of fruits and vegetables, each piece fresh and perfect, arranged with enormous care. And the olives! Great vats of them, shining black and green, at least twenty varieties, nothing like the bland ones that come in cans at the supermarket. The cheeses are next to the olives. You can feel your arteries filling up just by looking at them. And what if you were really hungry? I know that I feel quite sated after a walk through the aisles, stopping to pick up a loaf or two of my favorite German bread, the kind not to be found in more modest establishments.

My elegant market is one of my symbols for abundance, perhaps abundance in excess. Yet abundance comes in many guises. Most obviously, there is money. Possessing money is not aesthetically or emotionally satisfying, since most of our disposable income exists only on paper—or more likely nowadays in computers. This is a disappointing contrast to the world of fairy tales and pirate movies, where wealth was visible and tangible. Great chests filled with gold and jewels let you know what you had: abundance could be seen and touched, hidden and revealed. You could plunge into it up to your elbows and let it trickle through your fingers.

Then there is the abundance of material possessions, ranging all the way from precious art to just plain junk. I am conscious of my well-equipped kitchen these days as I think about downsizing. What started out as abundance now feels like a burden. There are twelve place settings of my grandmother's Haviland china, occupying an inordinate amount of cupboard space. I last used them for a Thanksgiving dinner in 1962 and then decided that they were altogether too much trouble. Life is too short to spend time washing fragile old dishes by hand unless one can see it as an exercise in contemplation—which I cannot. I'm planning to unload them on my older daughter as an act of family piety. Not quite junk but neither beautiful nor valuable are the serviceable lasagna pans that go back to the days when I entertained a houseful of starving college students. This required acres of pasta and at least four cakes. Now it's time for the cake pans to go too.

The abundance of creation is more mysterious than our accumulated "stuff," full of surprises, and quite beyond our control. There is the abundance of the harvest: right now I am eating ripe peaches at every meal, savoring them, and eagerly waiting to be inundated by tomatoes. The woodchucks in Jenkins Hollow have gotten plump, and the bears have filled out nicely after their long winter fast. The wild blackberries are flourishing, as is the poison ivy, a reminder that nature's abundance is not limited to the edible. Nor—by human standards—to the beautiful or the useful. This spring my city was swarming with cicadas. Dormant, having lived underground for seventeen years, they burst forth by the hundreds of thousands, the millions. They mated, deposited their eggs, and died, having enjoyed an active life of a day or so after that long wait in the darkness. They dropped from the trees, they flew into our faces, they climbed the walls of the houses, they covered the sidewalks. They were everywhere. I can recognize their abundance, but I confess my limitation when I fail to see beauty or utility in swarms of big, clumsy insects.

On the other hand, there is an abundance of beauty in nature that even the least sensitive can comprehend. Our neglected meadow in Jenkins Hollow is covered right now with waist-high Queen Anne's lace. A farmer would tell me that it makes terrible hay if I could find anyone willing to mow it. But it is beautiful beyond belief: a sea of lacy white flowers that are at the same time intricate and simple. I love to walk through it, even when I know that ticks are lurking on its stems, just waiting to find a new home on me. I can acknowledge the abundance of ticks along with the wildflowers, but I have yet to learn to value them.

I never leave my favorite art museum without a feeling of satiety, knowing that I have absorbed all that I can and maybe a little bit more. At the same time I have a sense of greed: I want it *all,* I want to immerse myself in line and color and remember every bit of it. Similarly when I stroll through a mega-bookstore, my hands in my pockets to restrain my acquisitiveness, I want them *all*—the novels and the poems, the plays and the essays and the biographies. The abundance of beauty in music, books, and visual art rivals the abundance of nature. My inexpensive CD player can bring me Billie Holiday, Andrés Segovia, and Dietrich Fischer-Dieskau—a feast—while I plod along at my desk, sometimes overwhelmed by the sheer abundance of words in the English language.

Words are yet another kind of abundance. I remember my delight when each of my children discovered speech. Suddenly they were differentiated from other lovable little mammals. They could name things, with ever greater precision. They could describe their feelings with ever greater nuance. In an amazingly short time, they had discovered the abundance of language. As a writer I seem to spend an inordinate amount of time looking for precisely the right word. I suspect myself of procrastination—why not just write something approximately on target and then think about it later? But the hunt for the right word can also become a journey through the enchanted forest, a treasure hunt where each verbal discovery opens new possibilities. This is an abundance that native speakers easily take for granted.

It is a salutary exercise to be a linguistic stranger, perhaps to have some idea of the richness of the discourse around you but not able to participate fully. Years ago, when I lived in Argentina, I acquired a useful but limited vocabulary of housewife Spanish. I survived, was in fact often complimented on my linguistic skills, but was saddened and made a little envious by the flood of words around me—powerful, melodious, inviting, but not really *mine.* I would struggle at dinner parties to formulate a sentence or two—*something* relatively germane to the topic under discussion. Then, just when I was ready to make my contribution, the topic would shift, and I would be left with a well-crafted sentence that sounded reasonably intelligent but would never be heard.

I found these efforts to develop a usable language even more poignant, and maybe a little bit frightening, not long ago when I spent a few days on my own in Beijing. An abundance of words surrounded me as I walked around the city: some sounded harsh, some melodious, all exotic. But they were not mine. I tried not to let myself think of my helplessness, at the very least my diminishment from an articulate person to a quite silent one. It felt like a cop-out to retreat to my hotel to watch English-language movies, or to permit the anxious concierge to send me out with a little printed card in my pocket: "If found, please return the speechless and foolish woman to the Palace Hotel."

The abundance of words can be a treasure trove or a labyrinth of cacophony—it all depends. Certainly there are times when, either as a writer groping for the perfect word or an intimidated tourist who cannot read the street signs, I fear that abundance. Like Alfred P. Doolittle, I fear having too much cash in my pocket.

❖ *Holding All Things Lightly*
Doolittle and I both need to pay attention to the ancient concept of detachment, which runs like a thread through the classic writings of the spiritual tradition, from Meister

Eckhart's sermons down to the poetry of T. S. Eliot. Indeed, it is not a concept peculiar to Christianity, but echoes through the great spiritual traditions of the East as well: some passages of the *Tao te Ching* sound as if Eckhart might have written them. If we can achieve some measure of detachment in the midst of abundance, we are able to hold all things lightly. While we may never achieve the self-abandonment ascribed to the holy eccentrics of the desert, we are able to stop grasping, to still the anxiety that lies at the heart of acquisitiveness, and let go.

Attention and intention are important if we are to live at peace with abundance, to recognize the difference between greed and grateful acceptance. Greed holds on tight and always needs more. The children of Israel were fed generously with manna in the wilderness, but failed to recognize the munificence of the gift. We need to know the difference between sufficiency—which is to be savored, enjoyed, and shared—and glut, which deadens the soul. We need to remember that sins can cluster around abundance like flies buzzing around spilled honey. We all know what greed feels like: we want more and more, and we fear there will never be enough. Covetousness and envy often travel together: we cannot savor what has been given us because we are preoccupied with our neighbor's good fortune.

But there are difficulties. It is hard to accept that everything is a gift, to believe in our hearts that—despite the paycheck arriving regularly after hours of labor—nothing is earned. Think of the difficulty most of us have in accepting gifts. We feel the burden of reciprocity: if you give me something, surely I owe you. How can I pay you back? It is almost impossible to believe that some good thing could come to us with no strings attached. We may feel discomfort: I do not deserve this; I have not earned it; if I let myself rejoice in it, it might all disappear and I will be worse off than before. Our clichés betray us. Increasingly I hear, as a rationale for charging a fee for spiritual direction, "You only value what you pay for." Or another cliché:

"There is no free lunch." Maybe not in the hard world of the marketplace, but God sets a bountiful luncheon buffet and invites us all, deserving and undeserving, to partake.

❖ The Cost of Abundance

So what makes us uneasy? There is a bit of Alfred P. Doolittle in many of us: after all, if we have been richly gifted with tangibles or intangibles, we may have to do something about it. We may have to claim the responsibility of good stewardship, of living in awareness that there is work for us to do, of knowing that we have every good thing on loan. Maybe we feel called to deal abundantly with the abundance that has come to us, or maybe we feel constricted, paralyzed by our fear that we had better hold on to what we have before it is taken from us. Maybe we have lost the gift of celebration, if indeed we ever had it.

My Great-Aunt Matt, probably the least joyous person I have ever known, lived for nearly eighty years fearful of acknowledging God's generosity. I never knew whether she feared being struck down for pride or levity, or for the conviction that one false move would take from her what little she had. Whatever her motivation, she was a true sister to the fearful servant in the parable of the talents. If she had dared even to reflect on whatever modest treasure she might possess, she would have rushed to bury that one talent in her backyard. She could not even rejoice in good weather. I shall never forget her comment when rain was forecast for the Fourth of July: "Better they should have to stay home than go driving around and get broken legs"— "they" being anyone so foolhardy as to accept the gift of a summer holiday at face value, those who dared to assume that it was permissible to enjoy a few cloudless hours. Poor Aunt Matt! The sun never shone on her, regardless of the weather report, and she spent a lot of time burying her bits of treasure rather than driving around and risking a broken leg. Aunt Matt was perhaps an extreme case, but I cannot deny our kinship. That's probably why I always had a soft

spot for her, even as I dreaded interminable Sunday din-
ners in her company.

What do we fear? Do we anticipate loss even before we
have celebrated gain? Do we put our gifts away on a closet
shelf because they are too good to use, but we want to hold
on to them just in case? Only yesterday I added an elegant
handbag to my collection for the parish clothing drive. It
was a gift from over thirty years ago, capacious, made of
some kind of endangered reptile hide. I never used it; it
had sat on at least three closet shelves over the years, moving with me from house to house because it was always
just a little bit too good, too special to be crammed full of
files, calendars, paperbacks, and an extra pair of shoes and
dragged hither and thither on the subway. What else, I
wonder, have we put on our closet shelf to be used some-
day—maybe—but not now? Not just tangibles, like my
elegant leather bag, but all sorts of intangible gifts and talents? The gifts that we want to keep in mint condition, that
we do not want to risk marring, scratching, or using up
completely? If I put them on a back shelf of my soul, I can
forget about them for months or years. It's always a surprise
when I visit them now and then to see that they have
grown tarnished or rusty—or that maybe they have lost
their value.

Then too, there is the awareness of our own unworthiness. Abundance makes us anxious because we are sure we
don't deserve such bounty. Maybe it was all a mistake or
pure chance, and the good things of our life were really
meant for someone else. Maybe it is better not to enjoy
them or even recognize them, because they might be
snatched away. Or perhaps we feel guilt as we look around
us and see stark poverty—not the comfortable sufficiency
of monastic poverty but the degrading, spirit-killing priva-
tion that is the lot of the poor and dispossessed. What right
have I to live in such plenty? The very least I can do is to
refuse to enjoy my abundance by feeling guilty about it,

which presumably lets me off the hook of true compassion and right action.

The monastic ideal of poverty, which eschews individual ownership of anything, can point us in the right direction even in the midst of our surfeited culture. When the fear of not having enough in the future or that feeling of needing "just a little bit more" recedes, it becomes possible to savor the comfort of sufficiency in the present. When we are sure that there is plenty, more than enough for everyone, we can afford to be generous. Since all is gift, we can enjoy God's abundance even as we own nothing. Gracious acceptance of plenty is a challenge, calling forth in us both gratitude and humility, and our first step might be a simple "thank you."

Questions for Prayer and Pondering

❖ Schedule regular time with yourself for an inventory of your home, office, and garden. Don't neglect the cluttered garage and basement, nor the depths of the closets and cupboards. What is treasure and what is trash? Where is the line between sufficiency and glut? Which possessions sustain you, and which are unnecessary burdens? What are you going to do about it?

❖ Now look within yourself: where have you been richly gifted? or modestly so? Your inner abundance can be ignored or hoarded or lavishly given away in the comfortable knowledge that the supply is inexhaustible. What are you going to do about it?

15 ❖

Loving Generosity

❖ When I was about nine years old, in Mrs. Sommers's
Sunday school class, we sang the same song every
week: "If you want to be happy, give something away."
Musically, it was unremarkable, and I cannot remember
any more of the words. We sang it lustily, but did we
believe it? I most emphatically did not. I was not a child—
even as a very young child—to snatch others' toys. It never
crossed my mind to steal. But I had a strong sense of enti-
tlement, of what was *mine,* and I intended to hold on to it.
The idea of divesting myself of my humble hoard of toys
and books was absurd. But then, in Sunday school we paid
lip service to a lot of things that no sensible person could
possibly believe.

As a child obligatory gift-giving did not cost me anything. My dime for the Sunday school offering—don't forget that this was during the Depression when ten cents was
a substantial gift—was handed to me by my father on
Sunday morning to put in the little envelope that I
dropped in the collection plate. So it did not cost me anything. Ditto the modest birthday presents for my friends:
birthday parties were rare events, and the birthday child's
expectation of loot was limited. As for Christmas, Santa
Claus brought the gifts, so this let all the ordinary mortals

in the household—including me—off the hook. I was into justice and fairness, not the wild abandon suggested in Mrs. Sommers's uplifting song. If you had the good fortune to possess something, prudence demanded that you hold on to it.

In retrospect, I am stunned by the sharp contrast between the gospel message of lavish—and from my juvenile point of view, indiscriminate—generosity, and my innate cautious tenaciousness. In my defense, I would note that I was a child of my time and ethnicity. It would probably have been beneficial, indeed liberating, if my family had some drops of Mediterranean or tropical blood in our veins and a few troubadours and vagabonds among our ancestors.

Yet the insistence on generosity in the Hebrew Scriptures makes it very clear that works of charity and mercy are a sacred obligation, not simply a nice idea to be taken seriously when we find ourselves with a surplus. Those who have something of value—not just the wealthy but also those with a mere sufficiency—must care for the have-nots. The corners of the fields must be left ungleaned for the poor, and the fruits of the orchards and the vineyards left unharvested every seven years. When the poor had gathered enough, the animals were welcome to whatever was left. And, shocking as it is by today's standards of economic justice, debts must be forgiven every seven years. Of course, there was no credit card industry, and those living on the edge were not steadily bombarded with tempting messages to buy now and pay later. Nevertheless, ancient Israel was indeed a welfare state. No doubt some of the seeming unselfishness was really quite grudging, but it had to make a difference if the benefactors were responding to a divine command rather than the bidding of faceless (and possibly corrupt) bureaucrats.

Jesus, too, is emphatic about the sacred duty of generosity in his parable of the king who judges the actions of his people. Similar to stories told in many cultures in which the king or god moves among his people incognito, rewarding kindness and generosity and punishing cold-heartedness, Jesus' version inspires awe. "Lord," ask those about to be judged, "when did we see you hungry or thirsty or a stranger or naked or in prison?" The answer, of course, is terrifyingly simple: "Just as you did not do it to one of the least of these, you did not do it to me." The "least" can have many meanings: the poor, the foreigner, the disabled, the widow, the child, the prisoner, the shift-less, the addict, the mentally ill, the undeserving. Why, after all, could they not be expected to care for themselves?

It is a powerful, simple story, one of the gospels assigned to the feast of Christ the King. I have heard sermons preached on this text and even preached a few myself; I confess with shame that I move swiftly and lightly over the last sentences of the parable. After all, on the Sunday before Advent, we are beginning to think about Christmas, and the ending to this story is inexorable.

> Then he will say to those at his left hand, "You that are accursed, depart from me into the eternal fire prepared for the devil and his angels; for I was hungry and you gave me no food, I was thirsty and you gave me nothing to drink, I was a stranger and you did not welcome me, naked and you did not give me clothing, sick and in prison and you did not visit me." . . . And these will go away into eternal punishment, but the righteous into eternal life. (Matthew 25:41–46)

This is radical stuff! The stakes are high. How can we hear it, read it, and not take it seriously?

We twenty-first-century Christians are not the only ones to struggle with fundamental questions of stewardship and sharing from our abundance. In one of his sermons the fourth-century bishop Basil the Great brought his hearers up sharply:

What keeps you from giving now? Isn't the poor person there? Aren't your own warehouses full? Isn't the reward promised? The command is clear: the hungry person is dying now, the naked person is freezing now, the person in debt is beaten now—and you want to wait until tomorrow? "I'm not doing any harm," you say. "I just want to keep what I own, that's all." You own! You are like someone who sits down in a theater and keeps everyone else away, saying that what is there for everyone's use is your own. If everyone took only what they needed and gave the rest to those in need, there would be no such thing as rich and poor. After all, didn't you come into life naked, and won't you return naked to the earth?

Basil then concludes with words that go to the heart of our assumptions of ownership:

> The bread in your cupboard belongs to the hungry person; the coat hanging unused in your closet belongs to the person who needs it; the shoes rotting in your closet belong to the person with no shoes; the money which you put in the bank belongs to the poor. You do wrong to everyone you could help, but fail to help.

❖ Works of Charity and Mercy

So works of charity and mercy are not optional. The very word "charity" all too often has negative or at least misleading connotations of compulsion and condescension: we give to the needy because we are compelled or at least pressured by some authority. No wonder that, in my working days, I was always cranky at fund drives for worthy causes. I did not actually begrudge a modest contribution to help the poor or save the rain forest, but I resented even the mild coercion of the emphasis on *one hundred percent* participation from the office. I usually ended up conforming, but there was no love in my charity.

Moreover, charity as the world understands it is hierarchical: the giver can feel great self-satisfaction in his generosity while the recipient is expected to be properly grateful. Again, there can be no condescension in true charity. I keep forgetting this in my encounters with the homeless in our neighborhood. When I offer a dollar (along with a little lecture about the ecumenical social service office just up the street), I find myself expecting lavish expressions of gratitude and realize with chagrin that I may, after all, be a bit of a fake. Condescension can feel very pleasant, but only if the recipient agrees to follow the script. The recipient of our generosity must, in the words of my grandmother's generation, know his place.

Maybe this is where mercy enters in, assuring that our giving is a work of true charity, for mercy is a generous, nonhierarchical virtue. "Blessed are the merciful," Jesus tells us, "for they will receive mercy." The prize here: if we are merciful, we will receive mercy—and we never know when we might need it! Never know when we might be broken, needy, overwhelmed, and helpless. It is precarious, indeed dangerous to assume that we graciously bestow mercy upon others, but will never be in their position. Then we are not merciful; rather, we are patronizing and caught in self-delusion.

Mercy requires that we *do* something: we might feel compassionate, but we cannot truly be merciful until we act on our feeling. The recipients of our mercy may not "deserve" our generosity, indeed most often they do not, at least by the world's standards. As a people, we are very much into balance, making sure that everything adds up and that we get our money's worth—if only in properly expressed gratitude. Mercy, however, is an untidy virtue that refuses to keep score.

Our theological tradition has given us a catalog of gifts that are the corporal and spiritual works of charity and mercy. The former are almost identical with the acts of loving generosity enumerated by Jesus in his parable of the

Last Judgment: feeding the hungry, giving drink to the thirsty, clothing the naked, harboring the stranger, visiting the sick, ministering to prisoners, and burying the dead.

It is hard not to be aware of the need for mercy in the world, well-nigh impossible not to be touched by the plight of the sick, the hungry, the naked, and the prisoner, whether they live in our own community or halfway around the globe. Our senses are assaulted by the media, and—for the most part—Christians and others *try* to respond to the visible suffering in the world, to ease it as we can. So we support food and shelter programs, distribute clothing, maintain prison ministries and assorted chaplaincies. These are all good works. But it is clear that we are also called to more subtle acts of mercy: to be present to the spiritually hungry and thirsty, spiritually to clothe those stripped of dignity, to be present to those whose sickness is not bodily and whose prisons are invisible.

This is a much more difficult work. Writing a check is not enough. Sentimental feelings are not enough, especially if we can turn them on and off. Even putting in hours of service at a food pantry or shelter is not enough unless our gift is offered with love. As Paul tells the difficult Corinthians, he can give away all his possessions, his very self; but if he lacks charity, he is nothing.

❖ *True Gifts*

We are commanded, compelled to be generous givers, prodigal in our stewardship of works of mercy and charity. What are these gifts? What distinguishes them from the obligatory exchanges that mark our quasi-official occasions of generosity? What distinguishes them from the exchange of gifts between equals?

A true gift is offered without conditions, nor is it necessarily "deserved." Will the beggar sitting on the sidewalk outside the supermarket spend my dollar on bread or booze? Once the money has left my hand, it's his; what he does with it is none of my business. We let go of it, with no expectation of reciprocity. Our works of charity and mercy cannot buy love or even gratitude.

A true gift is often costly. I think about this on the third Sunday of each month when St. Columba's sponsors a clothing collection. As I gather up usable garments that I no longer want—too long, too short, out of fashion, maybe just a little seedy—I feel quite virtuous until I remember that I am probably the chief beneficiary of my supposed generosity: the overcrowded closet is now much tidier, and I might even need to go shopping for replacements. Similarly, those grudging, obligatory donations— kicking in for the gift at the office or responding to the maddening pledge drive on public television—are not really gifts. In the deepest sense they cost me nothing, for they have not touched my heart. Instead, I am simply buying relief from annoyance.

A true gift is not always utilitarian, although mittens and underwear can sometimes be very welcome under the Christmas tree. The disciples and others around Jesus understood nothing about the lavishness of from-the-heart giving when they objected to the extravagance of the woman who anointed his head with precious ointment. "What a waste!" they complained. If the ointment had been sold, the money could have been given to the poor. They missed the point completely. Their reaction was neither prudent nor generous, but downright mingy. Charity and mercy are both extravagant virtues, holding nothing back and asking nothing in return.

One of my treasures is a ceramic frog, who sits by the fireplace in my study. No one could call it beautiful or dignify it by dubbing it an *objet d'art*. But it is one of the best gifts I have ever received. On a long-ago Mother's Day my three children pooled their resources to buy it at the neighborhood Sears store. I have no idea what negotiation took place as they decided why the frog and not a lace handkerchief or a bottle of cologne. Nor do I have any idea what it cost, but I know that their allowances were pretty modest. My little frog must have taken a big bite out of their liquid assets. My useless, ugly frog was a true gift. Had they bought me a new mop or a roll of stamps, I might have admired their frugality or their practicality, but I could not have cherished the present. My only dilemma now: who will be the recipient of the frog in my will?

Perhaps this is why I love to receive flowers. They are "good for nothing," a term of opprobrium applied both to persons and objects by those who worship utility above all. Just a few days ago my young friend Betsy came to sit with me for an hour in my little room at the parish and announced as she entered: "I've brought you a present!" When she produced an elegant little cloth bag with a Tiffany label, I was concerned. How could, should, would I respond to an expensive gift? What about reciprocating? Would I feel compelled to come up with a Tiffany-standard something? Then she emptied the contents of the little bag into my hand: seven smooth, white pebbles that she had gathered on the beach at the Scottish Isle of Iona, home to my patron saint Columba. She had remembered my love of rocks and had brought me a gift that was indeed good for nothing, but left me feeling very rich.

Betsy's gift set me pondering about the motives behind our works of charity and mercy. She wasn't paying off a debt or trying to keep our account balanced. The giving of gifts great and small can be rather like fighting over who picks up the tab for lunch, that familiar dynamic of "you paid last time, now it's my turn." God forbid that giving and receiving should not balance exactly! Which, of course in real life, rather like carefully orchestrated lunch dates, they never do. Betsy did not expect anything in return beyond my friendship. Nor was she obliged to bring me a gift because it was an officially sanctioned gift-giving occasion: it wasn't Christmas or my birthday, Mother's Day or Valentine's Day. The commercialization of generosity is expanding steadily. I will not be surprised sooner or later to find advertisements exhorting me to buy presents for my loved and not-so-loved ones to commemorate Presidents' Day.

I have said that a true gift is costly, not in dollars and cents perhaps, but nevertheless involving some sacrifice. What had my seven pebbles cost Betsy? Gathering them from the beach was not a sacrifice: she paused in a walk, stooped down, and picked them up. It was the work of a minute. So why was I so moved? I realize that, if she had brought me a little tartan-clad doll or some other knick-knack from a Scottish souvenir shop, I would have thanked her for her thoughtfulness and would have been mildly grateful, but not deeply touched. Sooner or later, I would have passed her gift on to one of my young friends or misplaced it and forgotten all about it. My handful of pebbles was a costly gift because it told me that I had been remembered thousands of miles from our usual meeting place, that in Betsy's thoughts I had been with her in this place of pilgrimage, and that she wanted to bring back just a little bit to share with me. In those rocks she also gave me a bit of herself. It was a gift of charity in the truest sense—a spontaneous loving act that brought her no advantage or benefits.

❖ What Can We Give?

Most obviously, our works of charity and mercy can be the harvest of the fruit of our labor. The gift of money can bring joy to giver and recipient, so long as it is given thoughtfully and lovingly, not to buy friendship or loyalty but proffered with open hands. It is a test of friendship to know when our help with college tuition or medical expenses can be received in the spirit in which we offer it. We can also give tangibles: a Tiffany bag with beach pebbles or diamonds, cars, and vacuum cleaners. I would not be thrilled with the gift of either the vacuum cleaner or the diamonds, but I hope that I could muster a gracious response.

We can also give the work of our hands: meals cooked, clothes washed, computer programs installed. Still more precious is the gift of time, which is really giving of ourselves. The gifts of attentiveness, compassion, friendship, and prayer for others are really an offering of our time: there is no shortcut. I rejoice that my hours are not billable, even as I grow in awareness that time is all that I really have and that it is limited—not because of a heavy load of obligations but because of my finitude. I'm going to run out of it one of these days. Perhaps the most difficult gift is forgiveness, even when it is not merited or asked for. This makes all the other works of charity and mercy seem ridiculously easy.

Jesus' standard of generosity is not the world's standard. "Just give a cup of cold water in my name," he instructs. So little and so simple as to be scarcely noticed! Like the widow's mite it is nevertheless a high standard. It demands that we live in awareness of the thirst all around us. Jesus said from the cross, "I am thirsty." Could he have anticipated that part of his suffering, assuaged at least a little by an unnamed person who offered him sour wine? When we are literally, physically thirsty, we cannot think of anything else. If we are deprived of water long enough, we die.

Perhaps our greatest work of mercy and charity is to offer that little cup of cold water to those who are spiritually dying of thirst. Maybe it is quite literally sharing a cup of coffee or a glass of wine, along with our gift of presence. More likely it is a refreshing sip of comfort, compassion, attentiveness. Maybe it is simply an acknowledgment that our brother or sister is suffering—not to fix anything but merely to be present.

Just as the merciful receive mercy, the giver receives gifts. For the prideful among us this can be a challenge. It feels so good to be the bestower of largesse, just as it is humbling to be the recipient of another's bounty. When I worked in a large nursing home, I was very conscious of the impoverishment of the residents. To be sure, it was a "good" facility: it was clean, the food was quite palatable, the care more than adequate. But the frail residents on the skilled nursing floor had very little: they were almost immobile, restricted to a tiny and coldly clinical space, and lacking even those small choices that make life pleasant— what they would eat, when they would eat it, what would they wear, would they sit up or lie down. I was especially fond of Gertrude, a tough old Jewish woman who long ago ran a newsstand on the Lower East Side. She always welcomed my visits. We would just sit together and talk. Sometimes she told me funny stories, and on the hard days she cried. As our friendship grew stronger, she would end each visit by giving me a chocolate bar. At first I tried to refuse, but then I realized that I must accept—truly accept—the role of recipient. I was younger, stronger, and highly mobile, but she had something precious to give me.

More recently I caught myself arrogantly rebuffing a friend's attempted work of charity and mercy. We were settling in for a weekend at a retreat house, an aging building with narrow, twisting stairs. I pride myself on always carrying my own suitcase, promising myself that when I cannot manage my luggage I will settle down and stay home. As I struggled—ever so casually—to heft my bag up and around the stairs, Amy started grabbing for it. I held on tighter. Finally, she exclaimed with exasperation, "For God's sake, Margaret! Let yourself be helped!" I let go immediately, realizing that, at least some of the time, it is more blessed to receive than to give.

These are some of the spontaneous acts of charity that can punctuate our days, small and not-so-small graced happenings that can sanctify the ordinary and enrich both giver and recipient. But intentional works of charity and mercy have their place in any rule of life. Just as generosity was required of the ancient Hebrews, our faith demands that we share our bounty with those in need, not just occasionally but purposefully. Membership in a parish, at least if we wish to cast our vote at the annual meeting, demands that we be "a contributor of record." During the yearly stewardship campaign we hear quite a lot about tithing and "sacrificial giving." I am never quite sure what to do with this. There are several ways of computing what a tithe might be, so if I juggle the figures carefully and take all allowable deductions, it won't hurt a bit. I am quite sure that more than this is expected of us. If we are to live out what we profess to believe, our giving will be generous, consistent, and really cost us something. One way or another, we will give something of ourselves.

Back when my blood platelet count hovered at an acceptable level, my most meaningful way of tithing was a monthly visit to the blood bank. The only cost to me, really, was two hours of immobility carved out of an otherwise busy day. (Harvesting platelets can take a long time.) I knew that the platelets were even more valuable than whole blood, and that mine were safe for premature babies and people with compromised immune systems. Of course, I never met the people who received them. Some of them no doubt recovered their health, and some of them surely died. But those little plastic bags of yellowish *stuff* were the best gifts I have ever been able to give. Now that my body will no longer sustain the regular loss of platelets, I am pondering what might be equally meaningful to offer—the ultimate gift without any strings. Paul, in his great hymn to charity, speaks of giving his own body. I'm not sure that I still have anything that would be useful, but I'm still looking.

It should be easy to give things away since in fact we do not own anything. In earlier times, when the gifts were presented at the altar, the priest received them with the words, "All things come of thee, O Lord, and of thine own have we given thee." I regret that we do not hear those words often anymore: it is good to be reminded of our own poverty, regardless of our bank accounts and stock portfolios. Awareness that all is gift can set us free to imitate the prodigality of a generous God.

If you want to be happy, give something away. I'm going to give it a try: next week I intend to give my complete set of *Calvin and Hobbes* to my nine-year-old grandson. That should make us both happy.

Questions for Prayer and Pondering

❖   Picture an old-fashioned scale, the kind with two pans that must be brought into balance. What is the balance between your weekly contribution to nonprofit organizations and charities, and those little extras that make life pleasant—a couple of trips to Starbucks and meals out when you don't feel like cooking? Has one pan sunk way lower than the other?

❖   Gifts from others cannot be repaid, but they can be passed on. What about the financial aid you received years ago when you were a struggling student? What about the hands-on help you received from friends when you were ill or coping with a fussy baby or moving? Think about all the gifts, tangible and intangible, that have enriched you. Then make a plan to pass them on.

❖   Check your mercy quotient. Charity offered without mercy can be harsh and judgmental. When have you, perhaps unwittingly, offered that sort of charity to others? On the other hand, our willingness to receive mercy means letting go of our defenses. When have you found it difficult to receive mercy from others?

16

Enjoying Authority

❖ "Authority"—a strong, heavy word. To wield authority requires decisiveness and willingness to act. "Author" is tucked away in the heart of it; if we dig down to its roots, we find that an author is not merely a writer of books but is one who initiates or creates. "Authority" is a word some of us find reassuring while others are a bit frightened by it, depending on our point of view and our past experience. When a justice of the peace performs a wedding, it is always "by the authority vested in me by the state" that he or she pronounces the couple to be married. Those few words certainly add gravity. Similarly, when we want to add weight to our gossip, we announce that we have it "on good authority." The presence and intervention of "the authorities" can be helpful or alarming, depending on which side of the law we find ourselves. "Authoritative" lends credence while "authoritarian" can bring out the rebel in us. So to accept authority is to accept the perils of power—our own, or the power we give to another.

The Bible makes it clear that the all-powerful God chooses to delegate authority. Adam, early on faced with the task of naming the animals, was also given dominion over all of them. Noah had responsibility for building the

ark—the LORD at least gave him explicit carpentry directions—but then he had the work on tending his passengers
on the ark during the flood. He had lots of authority—yes!
But it could not have been a pleasant job, and I doubt that
Noah enjoyed it very much. We are also told that "Jesus
taught as one having authority." Matthew tells us that Jesus
calls his chosen twelve together and gives them "authority
over unclean spirits, to cast them out, and to cure every
disease and every sickness." He then gave them extensive
and specific instructions, warning them that their work
will be hard and dangerous: "See, I am sending you out like
sheep into the midst of wolves" (Matthew 10:1, 16). The
disciples should expect to be arrested, brutally beaten, and
hated, Jesus tells them. There is no record that any of the
twelve had second thoughts or even raised a few questions
about what lay ahead.

So it appears that we, like the disciples, do not have a
choice. Whether we enjoy it or not, as Christians we are
expected, indeed compelled to accept our own authority
and that of others. Accepting the authority of others, when
it has been freely chosen, can be liberating. Even as we recognize our own worth and capabilities, it is a great relief to
know that the burden is shared and that we need not pretend to be all-knowing and omni-competent. We can
value ourselves more and live more freely when we know
our place in the great order of things. Like the servants in
many of Jesus' parables, we can know and accept the lim-
its of our own authority even as we accept the authority
of someone else. We can be as canny and resourceful as
they, knowing when to knuckle under and when to assert
ourselves.

But as free people, we enjoy a greater range of choices.
As a citizen I have to accept the authority of our elected
officials, even the ones I did not vote for. I have to file my
tax return, even when I would prefer not to contribute to
the national coffers. In other situations, though, my acceptance of authority over me has been freely chosen. As a

priest, I have willingly vowed to "be guided by the pastoral direction and leadership" of my bishop—even when I may not agree with him all the time. As the inhabitant of a vulnerable and aging body, I willingly accept the authority of my physician. I may know more about liturgics and literature than she does, but I have to yield to her expertise about bone density and blood pressure. These are humane and mutually respectful relationships, not groveling submission to tyranny. They are a sign that I know my needs and my limitations.

It is often easier to accept the authority of others than to claim our own. Perhaps we resist because we have been socialized to be self-deprecating. Certainly, women of a certain generation were trained to be self-effacing, to deny their gifts and their strong urges to lead and to compete. I think of this whenever I look at the pitcher painted by my grandmother more than one hundred years ago. It is a lovely piece, with roses expertly wreathed round it. As I hold that old piece of china in my hand, I remember my intense, inwardly rebellious grandmother who—if she had felt free of social strictures—would probably have painted pictures just as intense and angry as she was, all strong colors and bold lines. But as a good and compliant (outwardly at least) woman of her time, painting roses on china was the best she could do. The issue of her own authority, accepted or rejected, probably never occurred to her.

It is tempting to renounce our own authority voluntarily as well. After all, if we are helpless and impaired, either from circumstances or the hurtful actions of others, we cannot possibly be expected to do much beyond exist. I suspect that we have all known people like the invalid who had languished by the pool of Bethsaida for thirty-eight years, ostensibly seeking healing from its miraculous waters but unable to pull himself together to travel those last few feet. Who could possibly expect anything from him? He was no more than a nuisance, an obstacle to be stepped around by those with energy and vision to be going somewhere.

Maybe he had not wanted to be healed after all, but Jesus, with his brisk command to get up and get moving, disturbed a quite workable arrangement that had made no demands upon the sick man.

We can also reject authority because we wish to avoid commitment. It is so much easier to wait until the job—whatever it is—has been done and then to critique it. My great literary epiphany, the day I suddenly knew that I could actually read, was the story of the Little Red Hen. It is a story about the work ethic: the industrious little chicken finds some wheat, plants it, and harvests the grain. All her barnyard companions stand around, watch her work, and refuse to help; then, of course, they turn up to join in the feast when the grain is harvested. I imagined all the animal colleagues offering advice on how the work might be done better, what mistakes the Little Red Hen had committed, how they might be remedied, and on and on *ad infinitum*. We all know people like this, too; we have served with them on committees, helped them organize the parish festival, and assisted them in keeping the Cub Scouts running.

Timidity and the fear of failure can also hold us back from exercising authority. The status quo is safer. As an extremely cautious child, I remember my initial reaction to the parable of the talents, in which Jesus tells the story of a wealthy man who entrusted his money to three of his slaves while he went on a journey. Two of them were willing to accept the authority placed upon them and realized that it was not enough simply to guard the considerable sums in their care. So by shrewd investments they doubled the amount. When their master returned, he was so delighted with their initiative that he promoted them to positions of greater responsibility. The third slave, however, who had been given only one talent, was afraid of his master's anger lest he lose it, so he hid the coin in the ground. The master was furious and berated him: "You wicked and lazy slave!" No promotion for him—he had missed the point in a big way.

When I first read this story, I just couldn't figure Jesus out. He was behaving in a way completely contrary to the conservative values of my little world. I always identified with the careful fellow who buried his one talent—I pictured him tucking it into a Campbell's soup can for safekeeping before he buried it in the backyard. At least, with no margin to fall back on, he was not risking the loss of all that he had. I would have expected his master to say something like, "Good work! I knew that I could trust you. You were right to wait for instructions. You might have lost it or squandered it or fallen for some kind of get-rich-quick scheme. I wish that I had more people like you working for me." From my adult perspective, however, I can better appreciate the radical challenge of the story. It is indeed a call to risk, not foolishly but boldly. Even though part of me still thinks it might be safer to bury that coin under the lilac bush where nothing can happen to it, I know that when authority is placed upon us, we have to respond whether we like it or not.

A false sense of humility can impede us. We have all met people who insist on their own nothingness, who stop just short of saying, "I'm a worm, step on me." I find myself impatient when I am thrown together with these folk; I suspect them of being devious and manipulative, which they probably are not. More likely, they fear a robust assertiveness. Even sadder, they are probably convinced of their own unworthiness and incompetence. Worst of all, I can see bits of myself reflected in their self-deprecation.

❖ *Naming Our Gifts*
We are more like those servants entrusted with the talents than we might realize, certainly than we might care to admit. It is difficult to be humble—in the true and healthy sense of the word—and it is difficult to be grateful. If we could manage to live in a state of total awareness and stop

each morning to breathe a prayer of thanksgiving for each gift great or small, it would probably be mid-afternoon before we got up from the breakfast table. Just think about it: God has brought us safely through the night. We have rested—at least most of us have, and even insomniacs get more rest than they usually acknowledge. Our dwelling has not blown away or burned down or been washed away in a flood. Most of us manage to get upright and plant our feet on the floor. We have clothes to put on—clean clothes, not too shabby. Clean water flows from the tap when we brush our teeth. And we *have* teeth. And toothbrushes. And so on.

It is an edifying exercise to look deep within ourselves and claim our authority by naming our gifts. If we remember that we have done nothing to earn them, then we can let go of the mistaken notion that we are boastful when we claim them. I have occasionally pondered creating a new rite of confession, one where the "penitent" candidly, without apology or equivocation, names her gifts. At the end of the recitation of the list, the priest might ask, kindly but probingly, "Is that *all?*" It's harder than you might think.

But, of course, once we have named our gifts, we have to accept the responsibility and authority that accompany them. We are expected to do something with what we have been given. Unexercised muscles atrophy; hoarded treasure is corrupted by moth and rust. We might forget where, precisely, in the backyard that precious coin lies buried.

Not all our gifts are material; indeed some of the most important are quite intangible. They are our talents. That's what the parable is all about—not money management but our responsible and generous use of all that we have been given. Originally a standard measurement of weight in the Middle East, the talent by Jesus' time was a valuable coin. The slaves were entrusted with money, but for us, a talent is a natural endowment, a gift of intelligence, creativity, and ability. Our talents are our most valuable resources. Like all true gifts, they are unearned. Like all true gifts, they can go unrecognized and be wasted. Our talents, along with the authority to use them, have been entrusted to us; we have the use of them, but they are not ours. We have God's gifts on loan. They come with strings attached.

If we are not only to accept but to enjoy all that has been entrusted to us, then we must accept the authority that goes with it. We must be willing to risk—to risk failure, looking foolish, or having to acknowledge that we need help. A spectacular failure, along the lines of a fall from heaven in the style of *Paradise Lost,* can be easier to live with than the appearance of ineptitude or stupidity. We have to risk speaking up. It is so much easier to go along and then complain about the results when our great ideas—never spoken aloud, of course—have not been implemented. It is hard to fail when we let ourselves blend into the crowd. There were probably a lot of good people lining the road to Golgotha who watched and said nothing, even as they deplored what was happening. Peter, cowering by the charcoal fire in the courtyard, Peter the rock upon whom Jesus would build his church, did not do well at all on that first test of his ecclesial authority. I know that I sometimes find it easier to fall back on whatever diminished status comes to hand than to stand tall, accept my God-given gifts, and claim the authority that goes with them.

When we let ourselves enjoy the authority that is intrinsic to our Christian identity, we can be quietly emboldened to speak out against anything that diminishes others. So long as we speak the truth in love, we can risk making people angry with us. We can risk dreaming big dreams. We can enjoy the company of our fellow dreamers—because we are not the only folk gifted with authority—and we can generously recognize and honor their gifts. Thank goodness we don't all have the same gifts! I thought about this the other morning, as I stood with my coffee watching the weekly trash pickup from my kitchen window. The men moved swiftly, even gracefully. They did not drop anything. Their bodies were strong. The team moved in sync and got the job done with remarkable speed. They worked as people with authority: they knew what they were supposed to do and they did it. In the great inventory of gifts in his first letter to the Corinthians, Paul did not mention the people who cleaned up the streets of Corinth—though, to be fair, he was writing about spiritual gifts. They are important, of course, but we neglect the humbler gifts—the ordinary, everyday ones—to our peril.

Questions for Prayer and Pondering

❖   What are your gifts? It is a good idea to write these down as they occur to you. Let your imagination and memory range freely. Some of the gifts are material: enough money, a comfortable place to live that is warm in the winter and cool in the summer, adequate food and clean water, adequate clothing. Some of the gifts are people: family, friends, congenial fellow workers, wise supervisors who respect and value you. Don't forget good health. If your health is not so great, what can you find good about it?

Then your list gets much more personal: these are the "interior gifts" that other people may not always recognize or name. Think about your skills and abilities. Are you a good leader? a good follower? excellent at dealing with many details? or able to see the big picture? an eloquent speaker? a good listener? compassionate? generous? a wise asker of questions? What about you brings delight to God?

❖   How have you claimed these gifts? Have you thanked God for them? How have you accepted the responsibility to use them wisely and generously? How have you used the authority that your giftedness brings with it?

❖ What about those who have authority over you? Have you remembered to give thanks for their guidance? Have you accepted their leadership with an open heart? Or have you been guilty of the "evil of murmuring" or downright resistance?

❖ What about the balance of authority between you and others in your household? your workplace? the organizations you support? Where are the areas of disproportion? What feels just about right?

17

Holding Power Lightly

❖❖ How, as we exercise authority—not grimly, but with generosity and joy—do we walk that delicate line between authority and power? "Power," a word often heavy with negative connotations, is not typically associated with the spiritual life. But the presence of power in our world and in our lives is inevitable, and power *per se* is neutral, neither good nor bad.

As I write, the East Coast is bracing for the first of the late summer–early autumn storms. In a terrible (and I use that word on purpose) way, it will be beautiful. Lightning will slash across the sky. The giant oaks in my neighborhood will sway like willows. The noise of the wind and thunder will drown out all gentler sounds. The rain will fall in torrents. And there will be nothing for us to do except to take cover, wait it out, and hope that the basements in our solidly built houses do not flood and that the electric power does not go out.

Electricity is another kind of power, one that I foolishly think I can control by turning on a switch and paying the monthly bill. It humbles me to reflect on my reliance upon the invisible, taken-for-granted power that supplies our energy. Fossil fuel flies the planes that take me all over the world. It heats and cools my house. Electricity—I confess that I am not even sure of its sources—boots up my computer and does my laundry. My standards of personal cleanliness would change drastically if I were reduced to beating clothes on rocks in a river, assuming one were nearby: the Potomac is neither accessible nor attractive for this purpose.

Power buys me time as it renders myriad ordinary tasks quite effortless. Power brings light in the darkness and extends my day for as long as I can keep my eyes open. When I read late at night, I find myself thinking of Teresa of Avila, who must have written her books by candlelight, after she had finished her day's work. Or for that matter, I think of my great-grandmothers, for whom needlework was a restful luxury after a hard day's labor on the farm. A kerosene lantern was nothing like the clear focused light that shines on the pages of my book.

My mind is not big enough to begin to contemplate the enormity of nuclear power. So how can I begin to grasp the omnipotence of God? Yet all our prayers of adoration—and the psalms are full of them—remind us of the omnipotence of God and our littleness. So every day in my morning prayers, I express my adoration of the God of infinite power. When I let the words sink into my consciousness, I am not at all sure that I am comfortable with a God of absolute, total, unimaginable power. There are times when I would prefer a God who could be brought round to my point of view, or to whom I could at least offer advice. Yet a powerless God, a God of limited power, is not really worth bothering with.

For us fallible humans the exercise of power, like the wielding of authority, has its attendant dangers. Benedict recognized this and instructed the abbot—who had great, indeed, total power in the monastery—never to lose sight of his enormous responsibility and the accountability that accompanied it. Moreover, Benedict advised in his Rule, the abbot should never forget his own limitations, but "keep his own frailty ever before his eyes" (chp. 90).

When my children were very small, it never occurred
to me to compare my role of omnipotent parent with that
of a medieval abbot—but there were clearly parallels.
Although it does not last forever, the power of the parent
over the infant and small child is absolute. I suspect that the
horror that grips us when, all too frequently, we hear of
abuse or criminal neglect of children is at least in part a
reaction to our own experience and our own complicated
and ambivalent feelings about the role in which we unex-
pectedly find ourselves. When an infant cries 24/7 and
refuses to be comforted, rational judgment becomes
impossible and the imbalance of roles is forgotten. Why
isn't this ten-pound screaming little creature grateful?
Doesn't he realize all that I am doing for him? Doesn't he
know that I'm exhausted? Does she know that it's three in
the morning and we've both been up for hours?

Even mothers who would never harm their children
have felt pushed to the edge. They would never have
dreamed that they could be angry at the new little person
whom they love so much. Now they are burdened by their
power and frightened of it. They can easily sympathize
with Moses, who complained to God that the Israelites
were impossible, ungrateful, and totally out of hand.
Moses, furthermore, had it easier: God empowered him to
delegate seventy assistants. Only in retrospect, when life
had become less intense and demanding, did I reflect that
as a mother I had the power of life or death over my infant.
I can remember clearly those times, later, when the infants
had grown into small people able to talk and even to argue,
when I impatiently terminated all argument and discussion
with the proclamation, "Because I said so, that's why!"
Absolute power, usually exercised with benevolence, but
absolute nonetheless.

We can be greedy for power, or we can be reluctant to
accept it. In my book, those who lust after power are
immediately suspect. What can their motives be? Why do
they think they are worthy? Are they capable of good

judgment, magnanimity, and mercy? Can they be trusted to keep their own frailty ever before their eyes? On the other hand, my own reluctance to accept overt power is a cop-out; I would rather exercise power in a slightly sneaky, subversive way. Who, me? I'm just a good listener . . . a cook and bottle-washer . . . an itinerant priest, not even a rector! Yet I also know that I can, when the occasion demands, accept the challenge of power and run with it. Sometimes in the pulpit, sometimes as a teacher, sometimes by taking an unpopular stand on a controversial issue and then sticking calmly by it. Sometimes the greatest challenge is to acknowledge my own mistakes without defensiveness, aware that a bit of humility does not diminish me. Like Benedict's ideal abbot, we need to remember who we are in God's great economy.

When we give power to others, sometimes we want to go limp and surrender. In his youth my cat enjoyed games of chase and pounce throughout the house until suddenly it became too much for him. Then he would drop to the floor, all the starch and fight gone out of him, and wait for me to pick him up and tell him that all was well and that he was a splendid cat. I feel like that sometimes—it is tempting to give up, give over, and let oneself be cared for. Hence our eagerness to give power to those with whom we find ourselves in intimate professional or spiritual relationships: physician and patient, psychotherapist and client, priest and penitent, spiritual guide and seeker.

In my work as spiritual director, which I increasingly see as a ministry of simply hanging out with fellow seekers, I can see the perils that constellate around the issue of power. Too many folk are eager to be judged, scolded, and told what to do, and I see how easily this sacred work could become a way to gratify my own ego. It would be so easy to tell Sue, unhappy in a failing marriage, "Why don't you leave that husband of yours? I can't understand why you haven't figured this out yourself." Or to tell Rob, "You're wasted in that job—why don't you quit?" The writers of advice columns and the television and radio "personalities" who freely offer counsel seem to have no trouble accepting the power bestowed on them. Since I lack their certainty and maybe their relish for power, "Care for yourself" and "Why not pray about it?" is as far as I can safely go in telling others what to do.

But we can also exercise power over others by encouraging unhealthy dependence, by being too helpful, by being tirelessly omni-competent. My favorite British television comedy is *Keeping Up Appearances,* in which the social-climber Hyacinth terrorizes her timid neighbor in what should be a sociable coffee-drinking session at her kitchen table. Elizabeth drops her coffee cup, gets crumbs on the table, and sits in the wrong chair (after being invited "to just sit anywhere, dear"). By the time the coffee has been drunk, she is a trembling wreck. The scene occurs again and again, in almost every episode, and is hilarious. But when I look at it with a critical eye, I can see it as a cruel exercise of power by someone who knows how to choose her victim and, in the guise of hospitality, manages to make her miserable. Something tells me that this dynamic is not confined to the BBC.

There is also the subtle, masked power of the weak over the strong. The tasteless jokes about demanding mothers who keep their adult children emotional prisoners are about this manifestation of unhealthy power. To be told, "Don't worry about me, I'll just sit here in the dark, you go on and have a good time," is enough to dampen even the most exuberant spirits. The frail old can tyrannize the young, the demanding young can exert power over the parent struggling to make ends meet, the sick can manipulate their caregivers. My own mother, who enjoyed poor health for decades but made it to eighty-six, was wont to say, as we dismantled the Christmas tree, "Well, I wonder where we'll all be this time next year." I was well into middle age before it occurred to me that she probably wasn't actually going to die in the next weeks or months.

❖ *Power and Accountability*

So power is a fact of human life, wielded generously or selfishly, justly or unjustly, wisely or foolishly. I am learning to recognize it as a gift, even to enjoy it, all the while remaining aware of its perils. A clerical collar gives me power: people who do not know me very well are eager to attribute wisdom and holiness all by virtue of a rigid strip of white plastic around my neck. A title on the door of my office or my name on the big board out in front of the church can have a similar effect. A degree or two after one's name is also effective. When I was teaching in Hong Kong in a Chinese Christian community where age was a sign of authority and wisdom, even my white hair was a source of power: I could feel myself getting stronger and wiser by the moment. Fortunately, I returned home before I was completely seduced by it.

The line between using power with joy and being seduced by it is a thin one. The danger is lessened if we live in awareness of our accountability and, perhaps more importantly, commit ourselves to be accountable to another person. Spiritual and political leaders of our own time might do well to emulate the practice of the early Celtic Christians, who inherited from their Druid fore-bears the concept of the *anamchara,* the soul friend. Those who exercised power—chieftains and kings—were expected to submit to the authority of such a guide, to confess their transgressions and shortcomings, and then to accept judgment. Saints Patrick and Columba are reputed to have served as a conscience to their leaders. This was an intentional relationship, neither cozy nor truly mutual: there was no give-and-take. The contemporary ideal of spiritual friendship is considerably softer than the guidance offered in newly Christianized Ireland. The *anamchara* was empowered to impose some pretty harsh penances: severe fasting, pilgrimage (in those days you were not at all sure that you would return), and standing in a bog. I had not appreciated the severity of this penance until I visited Iona and let myself picture repentant dignitaries standing up to their waist in chilly water. What, I wondered, was the etiquette prescribed for this situation? Did one pass by the penitent community leader, pretending not to notice? Or did one commiserate, maybe ask, "What are you in for? And for how long?"

As the proverb says, "Anyone without a soul friend is a body without a head." This pops into my thoughts occasionally as I read the morning paper or watch the evening news. What would it be like if our heads of church and state were accountable to someone who wished only good for them but who would cut them no slack? Tough *anamcharas* of the Celtic mode are hard to come by these days, but finding someone in our lives with whom we can be openly, honestly ourselves is a tremendous gift. This might be a trusted friend, someone to whom, in the words of twelfth-century Cistercian Aelred of Rievaulx, we "dare to speak on terms of equality as to another self."[7] It might be the intimate circle of a prayer group. However we manage it, if we are to remain honest and accountable in the stewardship of our God-given gifts and power, we need to be in some lovingly distanced relationship in which truth can be spoken.

Occasionally family members and spouses can fill this role, despite the inevitable closeness of the relationship. My favorite example is Harry Truman, the U. S. President during the difficult years at the end of World War II and the beginning of the Cold War. He had to face his indomitable wife Bess each day as he returned to the family quarters in the White House. Regardless of the toadying, kowtowing, and bootlicking that might have taken place in the Oval Office, he lived with a formidable *anamchara* who happened to be his plain-speaking wife. Most of the time, though, spouses are simply too close to each other and need each other too much. We have to look farther afield for someone who can love us impersonally and speak truth even when we would rather not hear it.

✤ *The Power of Powerlessness*
Ultimately, however, whether we are the President of the United States or the head of the school board, an archbishop or the local police chief, we are powerless. At best, we have our power on loan. This is manifested to us in small things: the inevitable wait when the doctor is working behind schedule or we are stuck in traffic, the carefully worked-out timetable rendered absurd when the flight is canceled, the family picnic washed out in a downpour, the undignified, disabling twenty-four-hour virus that strikes us down just before an important event or meeting. Ultimately, our powerlessness is shown to us in our eventual diminishment and inevitable death.

And yet this is not really such bad news. Paradoxically, immense power lies in the acceptance of our powerlessness, of holding our power lightly and humbly. A long time ago a wise friend spoke to me of living in a state of "willing undefendedness." This is not at all the same kind of surrender offered me by my overstimulated cat who just wanted to drop out of the game. Rather, it is an open-handed letting-go, a free acknowledgment of powerlessness. It is a letting-go that can be offered with joy in the confidence that it does not really matter. Our minute drop of presumed power is nothing in God's great economy: it has come to us easily, even if we think it hard-won and well-deserved, and it can be relinquished easily. We can let it go because we are assured of something better.

Questions for Prayer and Pondering

✤   In what areas of your life do you wield power? How do you deal with your own powerfulness? reluctantly? prayerfully? with confidence?

✤   In what ways are you powerless? When have you experienced that powerlessness, in what specific circumstances—past, present, or anticipated? How did you deal with your own powerlessness? Can you accept it and respect it? When do you seek powerlessness as an escape or in a spirit of defeat?

❖ Is there a soul friend—an *anamchara*—to whom you are accountable? Do you know someone who wants or needs nothing from you, but who knows you in your gift-edness and your infirmities, who will speak truth to you in love? Do others turn to you seeking this kind of friend-ship? Are you able to accept the power they give you, aware of its sacredness and avoiding the temptation to mis-use their trust?

part 3

Getting Started

18

Building the Trellis

❖ Most of us already have an inner, perhaps unconscious rule of life that reflects our priorities and
preferences. We may not even realize this until we experience one of those days when everything is out of kilter—
the alarm clock doesn't go off, the car won't start, the
computer crashes, your two o'clock appointment is thirty-
five minutes late, and your spouse, child, or roommate desperately needs your full attention when you arrive home,
exhausted from a busy day at work. Such a day leaves us
disoriented and discombobulated. Like babies, who need a
great deal of consistency if they are to thrive, we need to
know what really matters, what we are about, why we are
about it, and where it fits into our day.

So many of us have found that it is quite helpful—
essential to our well-being, in fact—to craft and actually
write down a rule of life. The purpose of this rule is to
keep us clear and attentive, to enable us to live contempla-
tively in the midst of activity. The temptation, of course, is
to be overambitious and to set ourselves impossible
goals—and then to fail. I think of this as the "first week of
Lent syndrome": what begins as a bracing change of pace
and priorities turns into a real drag after about two weeks.
There is also the danger that the structure will become an

end in itself, so that our spirituality becomes joyless, life-denying, and self-centered. Particularly in regard to "spiritual disciplines," less is frequently more. A good rule can set us free to be our true and best selves.

Always keep in mind that a good rule of life is a *working document,* somewhat like a spiritual budget, not carved in stone but continually subject to regular review and revision. It should support us, but never constrict us. After all, we are not static creatures: we have times of turning outward and turning inward, easy times and painful times, times of intense activity and times of contemplation. Our rule—our trellis—needs to be adapted to how and where we are growing. It needs to be aware of where the good soil is to be found, when the rains might come and how to cope, which branches need to be pruned and which ones tenderly nourished and encouraged to grow.

Our rule should be practical, doable, and suited to our own circumstances at this very moment. As a freelancing empty-nester, I have much more control over my time than does the person with a nine-to-five job or a brand-new baby. Anything "spiritual" too often suggests being divorced from reality and can be the despair of people in the so-called mixed life—the mother with toddlers, the professional in a stressful job, the person who is working two jobs just to put food on the table, anyone suffering from a debilitating illness with chronic pain as a constant companion. We cannot be monastics, with our days structured around times of community prayer announced with a five-minute warning bell to remind us to drop whatever we are doing and turn ourselves to prayer. We are bound to failure and disappointment if we try emulate Benedict's monks too closely, and many contemporary religious orders are much more flexible than that.

The words "should" and "ought" are terrible tyrants. Again, we are bound to failure if we let them take us over. Our rule of life should support us, not constrict us like a suit of armor or a Victorian corset so that we cannot move freely or even breathe deeply. A fully armored knight knocked off his horse was rather like a helpless upended beetle, while Victorian ladies, at least of the privileged classes, seemed to faint a great deal. So our rule sets us free to stretch, to grow, to be our best selves.

❖ Writing a Rule

In crafting a rule of life, it can be helpful to look at four areas of relationship: our relationships with God, with the people whose lives touch ours directly, with all of creation, and with our own deepest self. As you begin to develop your rule, look for areas of disproportion and neglect within each of these relationships. Look for ways of being and acting that used to serve you well, but now feel arid. Look for challenges and opportunities for growth. Look for surprises. Look for areas of your life that feel pretty good, if not terrific.

As I have already noted, how we live out our relationship with God is the traditional part of any rule, providing the basis for all that follows. There are some pitfalls here: we might have unrealistic expectations of ourselves—as when we take on strenuous Lenten disciplines that become burdensome and constricting after the first few days. Or we can become rigid and mechanical in our devotional life: "Great! I've read Morning Prayer—that takes care of God. Now I can get on with the rest of my life." Or we can become so committed to the approaches to prayer outlined in our rule that we are afraid to stretch and change and try new ways of conversing with God.

This is a good time to ask ourselves: Why am I praying? Even more to the point: To whom am I praying? Ours is a God who calls us into intimate relationship, who delights in us and manages to keep on loving us even when we are unlovable. How can that awareness—if we are strong enough to accept it and savor it—shape the pattern of our devotional life?

Then we look at how we live out our relationship with others. What are our obligations of attentiveness and generosity to the people in our lives, especially those whom we touch directly: members of our household, family near and far, the person in the pew next to us or working at the nearby desk? Some of these are people we love. Loving relationships are not always easy: they can be clouded by conflict, grief, or worry. And, of course, we do not always love the people in our immediate neighborhood. What about the difficult ones, the incompetent and irritating ones, the ones who are impossible to like?

Here it helps to be specific. It may seem trivial for the rule of life to list a weekly phone call to an aged friend or relative, for a harried mother to pledge not to take out her impatience on her children, for spouses to deal gently with one another's exasperating foibles, but it is in the small, immediate, day-to-day moments of our lives that our spiritual life is challenged and matured. On a larger scale, we confront our struggle against contempt and coldheartedness toward those whom we so easily marginalize. Here, as elsewhere in the rule, we watch for areas of disproportion and danger. Where do we need to shore ourselves up? What must we watch for? Where are our pockets of sin, or at least the potential for sin? This is the corner where all the ugly little *isms* are lurking—racism, ageism, and sexism along with xenophobia, homophobia, heterophobia, and all the other phobias.

Then we look at our relationship to the world, to all of God's creation. We have been responsible for this area of stewardship since the very beginning: our first parents in Eden were given dominion over all that God had created. I would not presume to affiliate God with any of our political parties; nevertheless, how we exercise our franchise is a spiritual matter. When we are flooded with more information that we can absorb, how do we stay responsibly informed? How does our use of energy and water reflect good and thoughtful stewardship? Even how we carry the groceries home is a spiritual matter. At my old supermarket I gained the reputation of a crotchety eccentric because I so vigorously refused double-bagging. This is a difficult part of a rule of life: if we are honest with ourselves, we can usually identify our own small ways of sinful actions and patterns of behavior.

Corporate sin is harder to pin down. Here we have a more difficult time than our grandparents because we inevitably know so much more; we live in awareness of the inextricable connection of individual and the global community. I have a little crisis of conscience every time I buy a new turtleneck, knit by someone whom I will never see in China or Sri Lanka or Mauritius. Did it provide life-saving employment for someone who would otherwise have gone hungry, or was it the product of near-slave labor? I try to get myself off the hook by breathing a prayer for the factory worker, whoever he or she might have been, and hoping that I have not contributed to misery and oppression. Part of a rule might include thanking God that there are people in the world actively pursuing economic justice on a global scale and seeking ways to support their work.

Finally we look at our stewardship of our own deepest self. As we grow in knowledge of self, we grow in knowledge of God; similarly, as we grow in knowledge of God, we grow in knowledge of self. How do we care for ourselves? Challenge ourselves? Love ourselves, even as we work toward loving our neighbor? What do I fear? And what do I yearn for? To whom am I accountable? Is there a place for celebration in my life?

❖ Be Specific!

Now it's time to get started. I have found that it helps us to be specific: write your rule down in some detail, not hurrying but making it the work of several weeks. Since we are always changing and—I hope—growing, a rule does not need to be perfect or complete. Remember it is a provisional document, neither a constricting garment we can outgrow nor a rulebook to be consulted anxiously before every move. Rather, I prefer to treat my rule of life as I treat my grocery list. I organize it meticulously, separating dairy from produce, and baked goods from cleaning products. If I am feeling especially fussy, I organize the items according to the layout of the supermarket: fruit and vegetables along the near wall, meat and poultry in the middle, dairy along the far wall.

Then I go off to shop and leave the list on the kitchen counter. I already know what's in it.

Endnotes

1. I am indebted to Sister Agatha Mary, S.P.B., for her translation and illuminating commentary in *The Rule of Saint Augustine: An Essay in Understanding* (Villanova, Penn.: Augustinian Press, 1991).

2. *Ancrene Wisse* in *Anchoritic Spirituality,* trans. Anne Sacage and Nicholas Watson (New York: Paulist Press, 1991), 48.

3. *The Rule of the Society of Saint John the Evangelist* (Cambridge, Mass.: Cowley Publications, 1997), 119.

4. Quoted in *Cistercian Studies* (1973), 8:87–97.

5. See Joan Chittister, *The Rule of Benedict: Insights for the Ages* (New York: Crossroad, 1995), 153.

6. Ann and Barry Ulanov, *Cinderella and Her Sisters: The Envied and the Envying* (Philadelphia: Westminster Press, 1983), 91.

7. Aelred of Rievaulx, *Spiritual Friendship* (Kalamazoo: Cistercian Publications, 1977), 72.